MIND
of the
NATION

MIND
of the
NATION

Universities in Australian Life

MICHAEL WESLEY

LA TROBE
UNIVERSITY PRESS

IN CONJUNCTION WITH BLACK INC.

Published by La Trobe University Press in conjunction with Black Inc.
22–24 Northumberland Street
Collingwood VIC 3066, Australia
enquiries@blackincbooks.com
www.blackincbooks.com
www.latrobeuniversitypress.com.au

9781760643706 (paperback)
9781743823118 (ebook)

A catalogue record for this book is available from the National Library of Australia

Cover design by Tristan Main
Cover image: Maylim / Shutterstock
Text design and typesetting by Typography Studio
Back cover author image: Peter Casamento

As society goes, so goes the university, but also,
as the university goes, so goes society.

—CLARK KERR, *The Uses of the University*, 1995

CONTENTS

Ambivalence

AUSTRALIA'S UNIVERSITIES ENTERED the third decade of the twenty-first century secure and confident. Their total operating revenue of $33.2 billion had nearly doubled since the start of the century. While government funding represented $18.1 billion of this, universities were fast becoming less reliant on public money; revenue from overseas student fees and domestic student payments was set to overtake taxpayer funding to universities. Australia had more universities in the top 100 of the global rankings than any other country save the United States and the United Kingdom. Over one-and-a-half million students were studying at Australia's forty universities, one international university and one private specialty university, up from just over 800,000 in twenty years. More than half a million of these were international students, helping to lift international education to Australia's fourth-largest export sector and largest service export, generating $41 billion for the national economy. Chair of Universities Australia Professor

Deborah Terry told the National Press Club in February 2020,

> I know our best days still lie ahead. And that confidence is kindled every time we look at the constellation of brilliant student talent, and our inspiring young researchers. If you have any doubt about why universities matter, and the great force for good they are in the world, they affirm it.[1]

Three weeks after Terry's optimistic prediction, Australia's universities were pitched into the most profound crisis in their history. On 19 March, the federal government announced a range of restrictions on gatherings and travel, closing Australia's international borders the following day. Universities – institutions with a millennium-long tradition of gathering in close proximity students and academics from across the world – scrambled to implement the restrictions. Campuses that had begun the year as bustling, vibrant, crowded communities fell silent and deserted as in-person classes were moved online and everyone – students, academics, administrators – began studying and working from home. Terry's 'constellation of brilliant student talent, and inspiring young researchers' suddenly faced an uncertain future as universities contemplated the possible loss of hundreds of millions of dollars of international student revenue. As 2020 unfolded, many students faced crippling financial hardship as casual employment dried up; and as the lockdowns continued, the mental health impacts began to mount. Aspiring young researchers faced the closure of labs and indefinite postponement of research travel, while universities began to lay off staff in anticipation of major financial losses.

In a broader context, Australia's universities were in a better position to weather the COVID-19 restrictions than most other realms of Australian life. Many had been moving towards digital delivery of key aspects of their teaching for nearly a decade, recording lectures for later consumption, putting course outlines and study materials online, and providing easier access to digital library materials. University students and academics by and large had good access to computers and the internet and were among society's more sophisticated and comfortable online denizens. Systems of enrolment, class attendance, assessment and course administration had been moved online over the past decades. The move to doing *everything* online at the onset of the academic year was a wrench, unleashing a wave of innovation across the world, but Australia's universities remained functioning and in business, unlike other major elements of Australian life. Surely here was a cause for quiet celebration, an example of resilience, resourcefulness and determination to carry on amid the wreckage of the pandemic, right?

Wrong.

Australia's universities ranked among society's most prominent targets of passionate public and political argument during the COVID years of 2020 and 2021. This was an amplification of an already significant level of attention and controversy they had been receiving in earlier years, accused of political bias, intellectual conformity, crass commercialism and declining standards. Month after month, universities ranked with government, health systems and aged care as the institutions foremost in Australia's public discussion, subjected to heated denunciation and advocacy, condemnation and admonishment, in mainstream and social media. There was no easy ideological or social explanation for the commentary. Criticism piled in from the right and the left, as did exhortation and defence. Both government and Opposition criticised universities for what they were and weren't doing. In much of the commentary, there was a palpable sense of enjoyment that universities were doing it tough. The sudden loss of student revenue, crowed many critics, had exposed the rotten core of Australia's universities. The federal government refused to extend its JobKeeper payments for distressed businesses to universities, arguing that a period of financial hardship would force them to reform their 'unsustainable' business models.[2] It seemed that for many in Australian society, the COVID lockdowns were a perfect storm for Australia's universities, exposing their corporate greed, contempt for academic freedom and freedom of speech, shameless courting of foreign students, bloated corporate salaries, falling academic standards, architectural extravagances and intellectual arrogance. During the years of COVID lockdowns, a period when Australian society had more time to pay attention to media commentary and polemics, when the lockdowns and restrictions formed a social echo chamber shortening tempers and sharpening hyperbole, it seems we decided to focus significant attention on our universities.

This sits uncomfortably with the enduring image of universities in Australian life sketched by Donald Horne in his classic, *The Lucky Country*. In its opening chapter, Horne wrote that 'in a sense – Australia does not have a mind. Intellectual life exists but it is still fugitive. Emergent and uncomfortable, it has no established relation to practical life.' Australian society, he argued, was hostile to the sort of intellectual sophistication that universities furnished: 'The need to build up a certain kind of cleverness will cause great social tensions in all industrialised countries; but especially in Australia, where cleverness can be considered un-Australian.' For Horne, Australia's universities were marginalised; they were places where 'clever men nurse the wounds of public indifference.'[3] It seemed a stream of Australian public intellectuals heeded Horne's warning, taking off to make their name overseas: Germaine Greer, Clive James, Robert Hughes, Charles Mackerras, Geoffrey Robertson, Peter Singer. Against this backdrop, it is hard to square the passions that Australia's universities seem to rouse. Why would a 'nation without a mind', in Horne's words, become so passionate about its peak intellectual institutions?

The Silent Revolution

One obvious difference between 1964, when *The Lucky Country* was published, and 2020 is the number of people Australia's universities were educating. In 1964 there were 76,188 people studying at university in Australia – just 0.68 per cent of Australia's population at the time.[4] By 2020 there were over 1.5 million students at our universities, representing 6 per cent of the national population. Between 2000 and 2020, the number of Australians with a university degree rose by just under three million, registering growth of 146 per cent over two decades.[5] By 2020, 49 per cent of Australians aged between twenty-five and sixty-four had a tertiary qualification. Nearly 55 per cent of people aged twenty-five to thirty-four were tertiary educated, the ninth-highest proportion in the OECD (Organisation for Economic Co-operation and Development). In contrast, 36 per cent of Australians aged fifty-five to sixty-four had a tertiary qualification. Australia's proportion of tertiary-educated twenty-five- to thirty-four-year-olds is 18 per cent higher than the proportion of tertiary-educated fifty-five- to sixty-four-year-olds, showing the results of a remarkable expansion in university access in Australia (by way of comparison, the variance in proportions of tertiary education between these age cohorts is 7.6 per cent in the United States, 16.4 per cent in the United Kingdom, 14.4 per cent in Canada, and 12.4 per cent in New Zealand).[6] These figures tell us that, far from being marginalised, universities are playing a role in the lives of increasing numbers of Australians.

There is a silent revolution happening. In the space of a generation, Australia is being transformed into a majority university-educated society, begging the question: how will these high rates of university qualifications change Australia? Numerous reports have been written about how a university-educated workforce is necessary for lifting the productivity of the Australian economy. Attention has also started to be given to how education is shifting social and political attitudes. Thomas Piketty's analysis shows that widespread university education has created a 'Brahmin left' in Australia and in other Western democracies, transforming the support base of parties of the left from lower-class and lower-income voters to highly educated ones, particularly among younger demographics.[7] James Button has argued that the growing numbers of university-educated people has led to identity replacing class as the foundation for left-wing thought and action.[8] Bri Lee sees a different educational divide opening up, between the university educated and the non-university educated, based around condescension from the former and resentment from the latter: 'When the highly educated disagree with someone, their automatic response is to discredit their opponent, often in language that attempts to suggest their opponent is less intelligent somehow.'[9] Nick Cater agrees, observing the rise of a new 'knowledge class' which is 'insulated and isolated from the world of the educationally deprived' and has become 'a profound threat to Australian egalitarianism'.[10] In Britain and America, the education divide is thought to have fuelled the nativist–populist backlash against the elites in the form of the Brexit vote and the election of Donald Trump; Sam Roggeveen speculates that something similar could occur in Australia.[11] The 2022 federal election, which saw the Liberal Party lose six 'safe' seats in the country's most highly educated electorates, will no doubt lead to an avalanche of further analysis on the educational polarisation of Australian society.

What has attracted less attention is how Australians view the institutions that are firing this economic, social and political revolution in their society. One 2019 survey shows that nearly 80 per cent of respondents had confidence in Australia's universities, compared to 28 per cent for banks, 27 per cent for the federal government and 20 per cent for the media.[12] This is consistent with twenty years of surveys that show Australians' confidence in their universities hovering between 70 and 80 per cent. An interesting result, but one that tells us relatively little about more nuanced public attitudes towards universities. Confidence to do what? There is other evidence, however, that suggests Australians have three paradoxical attitudes towards their universities.

The first attitude might be labelled *agnosticism* – characterising a significant number of Australians who simply don't think much about universities. Universities appear to play a much less significant role in Australia's popular imagination than in culturally similar societies, such as Britain or the United States. In British and American popular culture, universities form a constant point of reference. Think of *Porterhouse Blue*, *Yes Minister*'s gags about the London School of Economics, *A Beautiful Mind*, Inspector Morse in Oxford, *The Social Network*, the Pixies' 'U-Mass', *The Secret Garden* – the list goes on. In Australian movies, television and music, universities rarely feature. The Australian idiom has no equivalent to the semi-ironic references made in Britain to 'a Balliol man' or Rhodes scholars, or the semi-reverent references in America to Ivy League graduates. Australia's universities, it would seem, are largely out of mind in our public conversations and culture. Government education policy certainly isn't a major political issue: the ABC's Vote Compass survey in April 2022 saw just 4 per cent of respondents nominate education as a top order electoral issue.[13] And, certainly, attending university does not guarantee lifelong affection or support for your alma mater. In 2021, one observer wrote: 'The current federal Liberal Party appears to be doing what it can to eviscerate the tertiary sector, yet the young Liberals in most states meet and recruit in those very quads under those very sandstone towers.'[14] The same logic applies to plenty of others in the parties of the left. Former education ministers John Dawkins, David Kemp and Brendan Nelson, as well as former finance minister Lindsay

Tanner, all agree that higher education does not have a significant impact on public opinion or voting trends.[15]

The second attitude is *aspiration*. The remarkable expansion of university education in Australia over the past three decades reflects surging demand for university places – much in excess of the growth of the Australian population. According to one study in 2015, the decade to 2025 will see a 34 per cent increase in the demand for university qualifications – although the pandemic may temper this.[16] Analysis by the Productivity Commission shows that during the period of the demand-driven system in which governments provided funding for uncapped growth in university places (2010–17), there was a one-third increase in the number of Australian undergraduate students, with much higher proportions coming from low socioeconomic backgrounds and government schools, and higher numbers of first-in-family university students.[17] This system, along with many other policy shifts in Australian higher education, was partly driven by anxiety over 'unmet demand' for university places; at times it was estimated that around 10 per cent of those wanting to attend university did not secure a place.[18] Prospective students and their parents tend to see university as a portal to economic security and social status, a perception particularly strong among migrant families.[19] Others suggest that Australians have developed an 'obsession' with attending university,[20] while studies show a significant rise in school and family expectations on young people to attend university.[21] As the new chair of Universities Australia, Professor John Dewar, put it in mid-2022:

Every year in the last week of February, hundreds of thousands of young people head off excitedly to Orientation Week at university to begin their journey to adulthood … They have one thing in common: people are proud of them. Grandparents, parents, partners, children. You hear it all the time wherever you go … 'My kid's got into engineering.' 'Mine's going to be a nurse.'[22]

The third attitude is *antagonism*, and it plays out through the media, political debate and social conversations. Universities, like all public institutions, should expect criticism in an era of falling public trust in institutions. What is striking is the level of emotion that infuses discussion of the state of Australia's universities. Apparently, according to our national newspapers, Australia's universities 'prostitute' themselves and 'cannibalise' others; they are 'addicted' to foreign student revenue and peddle 'destructive and nihilistic identity politics and cancel culture'; they are 'totalitarian' and 'willing to sell out the national interest'. Much of the vitriol can be appropriately attributed to the 'culture wars' – conservatives railing against the so-called 'woke agenda' of the political left – but by no means can this explanation cover all of the criticism hurled at Australia's universities. While voices from the right are raised over ideological bias, threats to academic freedom and the criticism of Australia's cultural heritage, voices from the left are vociferous critics of universities' corporatisation, the high salaries of vice-chancellors and the underpayment of casual employees. Then there are concerns about the high number of international students, the student experience, universities' financial dependence on China and levels of sexual harassment and assault on campus that come from across the political spectrum. Some critics point to university failures as leverage to criticise governments for not resourcing or regulating universities appropriately. Throughout 2020 and 2021, there were repeated calls for a royal commission into Australia's universities. The departing vice-chancellor of the University of New South Wales, Ian Jacobs, told an audience at the end of 2021, 'You have a sector here which is massively important for Australia, socially and economically, which is constantly under attack.'[23]

The antagonism is infectious. Student and staff protests have become part and parcel of university life, with anger at both university administrations and governments for what students see as deteriorating conditions at university. This anger often plays a defining role in Australians' experiences at university. Government ministers who visit campuses often do so at their own peril and under heavy guard. Education minister John Dawkins had a Coke bottle thrown at him during a visit to a campus to discuss his reforms. His successor, Brendan Nelson, was under close personal police protection for much of his time in the role.[24] Vice-chancellors are also often the targets of abuse, charged with being willing allies of governments that are intent on eviscerating the university experience. Following cases of chancelleries being invaded by students and the contents of vice-chancellors' offices being thrown out of windows, many university chancelleries now have heavy security barriers. Staff who work in them are used to going into lockdown as waves of student demonstrators encircle the building.

The Chemistry of Ambivalence

What is going on here? Australians, it would seem, rarely have universities front of mind but really want to study at them. They seldom write or sing about universities but get into angry debates about them. More and more Australians seek and gain a university education but don't think that much about them afterwards. And when they do, they are likely to be dismissive or critical. A rising number of parents want their children to go to university, but a vanishingly small number think that education is an important electoral issue. This puzzle about the role of universities in Australian life is important for several reasons. Our universities are modelled closely on British and American insitutions but have not established a relationship with society here that is equivalent to the role played by universities in those societies. And, arguably, Australia's paradoxical attitudes towards its universities has real consequences for society more broadly. Higher education policy in Australia has been made largely without broad public scrutiny or interest, and is immune from electoral consequences. Against this backdrop, it is easy for an antagonistic relationship between governments and universities to flourish. Universities' objections to higher education policy proposals are invariably interpreted as special pleading, and therefore evidence that the policy proposals are right. Sometimes it may be special pleading, but occasionally universities may actually be drawing on significant experience and expertise in pointing out the flaws in government policy. Public ambivalence about universities has and will continue to contribute to the sort of distant government–university relationship that leads to flawed policy, putting the institutions that so many Australians aspire to attend at risk of serious damage.

Ambivalence is the word that best seems to cover the paradoxical combination of agnostic, aspirational and antagonistic attitudes Australians hold towards universities. There are two meanings to this word, and both are helpful in thinking about the role of universities in Australian life. The more common use of 'ambivalence' conveys a lack of strong feelings either way about something, an apathetic shrug about what's being discussed. Most Australians, including those who have been educated by them, would seem to have little emotional engagement or enduring interest in the country's universities. It is an attitude that endures in the popular use of the word 'academic' to signify irrelevance, the opposite of the important, significant, practical. Attempts by universities to plead their case when they believe they are being targeted by punitive government policy usually have little impact. Until the 2022 poll, the ten most educated electorates in Australia were considered safe seats for the Liberal Party, seen by many in universities to be antagonistic towards higher education. A 2004 National Tertiary Education Union campaign targeting marginal Coalition electorates over the controversial university reforms of education minister Brendan Nelson backfired, seeing the Coalition's vote increase in most of the targeted seats.[25] This form of apathy suggests that many Australians see universities in largely instrumental terms, developing similar attitudes towards them as towards other service institutions. Global trends suggest that more and more people seek to attend universities for extrinsic motives – getting better jobs, making more money – than for intrinsic motives, such as fascination with a certain field, a love of learning or aspiring to become a more rounded individual.[26] Higher education specialist Andrew Norton's analysis of recent ABS data suggests this is very much the case in Australia, with more than 80 per cent of undergraduates citing employment-related reasons for attending university, compared to around 10 per cent attending for reasons of interest or enjoyment.[27]

But not all Australians are apathetic towards universities. As we've seen, large numbers of prospective students aspire to a university place (and their parents aspire to one for their children), while a significant number of Australians care enough to direct vehement criticism towards universities. The coincidence of aspiration and condemnation raises the possibility that the two opposing emotions are somehow linked. This points towards a second definition of ambivalence, 'the coexistence in one person of opposite and conflicting feelings towards someone or something.'[28] This form of ambivalence is explored by Sigmund Freud in his 1913 book *Totem and Taboo*. Freud argues that a dominant attitude, such as love or admiration, often has its opposite, such as hate or contempt, buried in the subconscious. When the dominant attitude is disappointed, its opposite emerges from the subconscious to determine the person's attitude.[29] Is it possible that some of those aspiring to university have high expectations of what they will experience, which are then not met, resulting in disappointment and ultimately negative feelings towards universities?

The Sublime and the Mundane

So much of the criticism levelled against universities carries with it implicit or explicit expectations of what universities should be but are failing to be. Reading through it, it becomes apparent that Australian society holds an ideal of the university as a benchmark against which it judges the current state of academia. Australia's first universities were founded for utilitarian motives – to provide the colonies with a professional class that would drive their development – but also to raise colonial society to higher moral standards.[30] Their founders also saw them as institutions that would preserve higher British ideals and traditions within the transplanted society.[31] Accordingly, the University of Sydney (founded in 1850) and the University of Melbourne (founded in 1853) each developed around gothic cloisters modelled on the ancient English and Scottish universities, whose architecture had drawn on medieval monasteries. Until the age of expansion of university attendance from the 1960s, Australia's universities were remote from society, the privilege of a narrow elite. It appears that many of the most vociferous critics of Australia's universities today have this view of what they should be: preserves of the sublime, humanity's highest achievements and ideals, kept insulated from the mundane concerns and motivations of everyday life. This duality appears to be similar to that observed by the great sociologist Émile Durkheim in the contrast of the sacred and the profane as preserves that are mutually exclusive in society, such that for the sacred to be contaminated by the profane is an act of corruption.[32] Contemporary critics of Australia's universities refer to them as 'the keepers of the nation's soul', 'once hallowed halls of enlightenment', the 'curators of Western civilisation' – ideals that have become corrupted by what universities have become. The polluting influence of the mundane comes in the form of steepling profits, corporatisation, overcrowding, declining standards and excessive progressivism.

The sublime ideal of the university endures in the Australian subconscious, fed by cultural currents from Britain and America. In June 1982, just as a massive surge in Australian aspirations to attend universities was getting underway, *Brideshead Revisited* screened on ABC television across Australia. Closely based on Evelyn Waugh's novel about a middle-class Englishman's involvement with a decaying aristocratic family, *Brideshead* sketched a glamorous vision of an otherworldly Oxford University in the 1920s. Directly quoting Waugh's text, the narrator, Charles Ryder, intones early in the first episode:

> Oxford, in those days, was still a city of acquatint. In her spacious and quiet streets men walked and spoke as they had done in Newman's day; her autumnal mists, her gray springtime, and the rare glory of her summer days – such as that day – when the chestnut was in flower and the bells rang out high and clear over her gables and cupolas, exhaled the soft airs of centuries of youth.

The series was an instant hit for the ABC, returning rare high ratings,[33] its publicity 'almost outdid the Royal wedding [between Charles and Diana] for sheer volume and style'.[34] The following year

Brideshead became the first television series released on VHS, its popularity hoped to promote the video format among Australian households, and the soundtrack sold strongly.[35] Interestingly, reviews showed the audience divided between those who loved it and those who hated it.[36] Either way, it penetrated the Australian public consciousness deeply.

The two lead characters, Charles Ryder and Sebastian Flyte, epitomised the sublime image of the university experience as completely uncontaminated by the mundane. They are immersed in high culture and bacchanalian living, surrounded by privilege and beauty, drawn to characters eccentric and passionate, completely unconcerned about money or career or consequences. Ryder characterises his experience as a rare and transforming rite of passage:

> I went full of curiosity and the faint unrecognised apprehension that here, at last, I should find that low door in the wall, which others, I knew, had found before me, which opened on an enclosed and enchanted garden, which was somewhere, not overlooked by any window, in the heart of that gray city.

There is little engagement with the formal educational experience in *Brideshead*, other than Charles doing enough to get through and an increasingly dissolute Sebastian failing repeatedly. For Charles, Oxford is socially rather than academically transformational: on his tastes, his attitudes, his social advancement. It is present throughout the series as a wistful memory long after he leaves: 'A door had shut, the low door in the wall I had sought and found in Oxford; open it now and I should find no enchanted garden.'

The ideal of the university as an institution of the sublime, a privileged, transformative experience, is drawn on by Australia's universities in their architecture, heraldry, ceremonies, marketing and publicity. Images of sandstone towers and cloisters, mortarboards and academic gowns, stately treelined avenues and clusters of students on manicured lawns are designed to tap into that subconscious ideal of the university in the Australian mind. It is triggered in the imaginations of both aspiring students and their parents, who either never went to university themselves or went there when it was a smaller, more elite institution. Higher education specialist Simon Marginson suggests that the steady expansion of access to university actually intensifies 'the need for definition and identity in the face of what are large, open and opaque higher education systems'.[37] Yet the scale of Australia's universities frustrates this need for recognition and identity. They are huge by international standards. If you divide the total number of students by the number of universities in Australia, it averages out to 36,579 per university; the same calculation reveals 13,740 students per university in the United Kingdom and 4,500 students per university in the United States.[38] Seven Australian universities are larger than the average: Monash University with 70,085 students; University of Melbourne with 54,579; University of Sydney with 54,048; RMIT University with 54,004; University of New South Wales with 47,891; University of Queensland with 43,698; and Queensland University of Technology with 38,678.[39] Detailed survey research over a twenty-year period by the University of Melbourne's Centre for the Study of Higher Education into the first-year undergraduate experience yields revealing perceptions among Australian university students. While 'most students were clear about their reasons for going to university, had a strong sense of purpose and identity, were excited to be at university, and were very satisfied with their course experience,' over time, later cohorts of students 'were less socially engaged in the university community, spent less time on campus, and more students tended to keep to themselves'.[40] Studies also pick up declining levels of application and motivation to study, linked to a disengagement from the learning process.[41] These studies reveal a gap between anticipation and engagement, between transformation and transaction, where disappointed expectations can blossom into dismissive or contemptuous attitudes – of students, parents and the broader community. It is a dangerous gap for Australia's universities.

Mind of the Nation

This book examines the complex, ambiguous, ambivalent place that universities, as increasingly consequential institutions, occupy in Australian life. It focuses on six aspects of Australia's universities where they sit at tension points of conflicting expectations and pressures in contemporary Australia. What they all reveal are significant gulfs between what Australian society sees and what universities want society to understand about them, between what higher education policy is trying to achieve and what roles universities should be playing in contemporary society.

'Money' tracks the evolution of the financing of Australia's universities. It is the starting point of an examination of Australian society's relations with its universities. It is in the seemingly dry and arcane field of higher education financing that we can most clearly see the nation's aspirations for higher education confront its unwillingness to pay for it. Australia pioneered a system of deferred student loans and became a world leader in exporting higher education as a way of meeting the gap between society's aspirations and its willingness to pay for them. Yet Australians seem increasingly unhappy with the entrepreneurial side of their public universities. Higher education financing reflects the evolution of government and public attitudes towards Australian universities and has played a profound role in influencing the nature of Australia's universities, which so often ignites passionate condemnation from so many directions.

'Value' examines Australian society's increasing insistence that universities should justify their public funding by demonstrating their contribution to society. Underlying this claim is a refusal to believe that there is an intrinsic benefit to society in having higher education institutions: value must be demonstrated anew and repeatedly. It examines a curious dynamic between Australian society and its universities: as universities strive to demonstrate their broader contribution, the public and government seem to become ever less satisfied or convinced by the value of these contributions. As a consequence, the growing role of universities has been accompanied by increased requirements that universities show how they are returning on taxpayer's investment. Driven by government policy, universities have reformed their internal structures to allow them to better deliver and demonstrate the prescribed forms of public value, relying less and less on collegial governance and more on hierarchic and competitive systems of resource allocation. The 'corporatisation' of the Australian university has alienated many – students, academics, families – while seeming never to quite satisfy those who are demanding the demonstration of their value.

'Loyalty' turns our attention to the process of academic globalisation that Australia's universities have undergone during the past generation, and the complex and often fraught public and government attitudes towards the results of this. Universities of course have always been internationalist institutions, powered by cross-border flows of talent and ideas. However, developments in technology, knowledge dynamics, government policies and academic incentives have hypercharged academic internationalisation since the early 1990s, and Australian universities and academics have been among the most avid and successful internationalists in the world. The ability to export education and form transnational research partnerships has delivered a remarkable strengthening of the Australian university sector, as can clearly be seen in Australia's strong showing in the global university rankings tables. But the pandemic exposed an underlying public discomfort with the effects of this wave of academic globalisation, as universities came under attack for having become excessively reliant on international students, and for partnering too assiduously with Chinese researchers. Academic internationalism has suddenly had to confront nationalism and geopolitics, generating the subliminal question: Whose universities are they anyway?

'Integrity' delves into the culture wars that have raged on and off campus over the past five years. The widening divide between those who see universities as the holders of the Western intellectual and cultural tradition and those who see them as vehicles for positive social and cultural change in society actually hides a deeper agreement between the sides on the role of universities in shaping Australia's social and moral fabric. What seems to drive the anger and animosity of both sides is a belief that in different ways, and from different directions, universities are failing to play this role. Controversies over academic freedom and the Ramsay Centre for Western Civilisation shows that what happens in universities matters deeply to those outside of them, but that hyper-partisanship and misunderstandings about what universities are and do is potentially very damaging for the role of universities in society. The answer to both sides in the culture wars lies in long-established academic norms and practices that need to be articulated and practised even more rigorously amid the deeply polarising debates and loyalties that have started to affect modern Australia.

'Ambition' draws our attention to universities' willing acceptance of a role at the centre of Australia's knowledge economy. As the twenty-first century is increasingly defined by the 'fourth industrial revolution', Australians are beset by both 'techno-optimism' over the potential of knowledge and innovation to transform economy and society and 'techno-pessimism', the worry that Australia will fall behind in the innovation stakes. A new logic of competition has followed for Australia's universities, which have reshaped their operations around research commercialisation, global rankings positioning and training a skilled workforce for the knowledge economy. These changes have caused significant anxiety within universities over whether they are being distorted from their true purposes and practices by competitive pressures. Externally, universities' successes and perceived failures seem to have had less of an effect on their relationship to Australian society than the universities expected.

'Privilege' explores a perverse outcome of Australia's push to broaden access to universities over the past seventy years. As the number of Australians going to university grows, higher education has become increasingly driven by prestige competition between Australia's universities and the students they attract. Along the way, variations between different types and missions of universities have been erased. Despite significant efforts by universities and governments to increase the proportions of people from disadvantaged backgrounds attending university, these groups remain significantly under-represented in higher education in Australia, particularly in our elite universities. Another perverse effect that has emerged over the past generation has been a large non-tenured academic workforce, creating a divide within Australia's universities between a secure, tenured academic class and an insecure and often marginalised class of casual academics. Despite widespread beliefs that higher education could be a driver of inclusion and egalitarianism in Australian society, we have ended up with a university system that reproduces and legitimises social stratification.

The picture that emerges from these six lenses on the role of universities in Australian life is complex and often contradictory. It draws heavily on research in higher education policy by specialists in many countries as well as recollections, conversations and personal experience and observation. The forces shaping Australia's universities and their relationship to Australian society have defined my own career. I began as a first-in-family under-graduate from regional Australia in a Group of Eight university the year before John Dawkins became education minister. I protested the unfairness of the introduction of student fees. I experienced the precarity of casual academic labour and still marvel at my luck in getting a tenured job. Later I watched with interest as more and more of my students were from overseas. I sat on panels doling out limited government research money in increasingly competitive programs. Most recently I watched the wrenching, debilitating effects of the COVID shutdowns on colleagues and students alike. In the process of researching for and writing this book, I have become increasingly convinced that universities have a strangely subterranean role in Australian life: they are central to so many aspects of modern Australia, but are rarely discussed, debated, examined. Australia's substitute for a public conversation about its universities, it seems, is the periodic reviews into them commissioned by governments and read only by a small coterie of higher education specialists and bureaucrats. This is not a good place to be, for our universities or society. This book is intended to provoke and open up a broader discussion about the role of universities in Australian life.

1

Money

WALK AROUND THE campuses of Australia's oldest universities, those founded over a century ago, and you will see a history of the fraught politics of university financing in Australia. Stylish sandstone quads and steeples, recalling the monastic grandeur of even more ancient institutions on the other side of the world, are crowded by ugly, box-shaped towers of brick and concrete showing clear signs of decay, despite their more recent construction. Then there are the new shiny constructions of avant-garde design: glass and gleaming metal, all tech-enabled and filled with creative spaces, proclaiming the university's place in the new digital innovation world. The architecture and materials in each type of building tell a story about the financing of higher education at the time of their construction. The old sandstone buildings were paid for by optimistic colonial or state governments flush with cash and eager to show their commitment to the finest traditions of learning; private wealth contributed to this vision and its architecture also.

The brick and concrete monstrosities can only partially be blamed on the rise of the brutalism movement in architecture; much more significant was universities' need to build new facilities to service rising student numbers but without the injection of resources to adequately service them. And the luminous futuristic edifices proclaim a new age of university wealth, generated by ever-increasing demand from international students and the healthy financial margins Australia's universities derive from teaching them.

Money determines more than architecture at Australia's universities. It shapes government expectations and university responses, university capabilities and student experiences, academic ambition and society's judgements. Money is the measure of universities' success and evidence of their moral failures; for some an enabler of world-class excellence, for others a corrupting influence that turns arcadia into soulless corporate greed. Money is the major lever used by government to shape what universities do; it is also the capability that permits some academics to escape teaching and administrative obligations, government requirements and reporting regimes. It is in the financing of universities that Australian society most clearly articulates its choices and compromises about higher education, its expectations and worries, its judgements about advantage and advancement. Money is the core of the mutual incomprehension between government and universities, in which each side cannot quite believe that the other can't see what it believes is patently obvious about university financing. The level of public funding for Australia's universities is used by some to castigate governments for failing to invest in the benefits of the knowledge sector, while for others government regulation creates a controlled market that permits university profiteering from the demand for tertiary credentials.[1] Former federal education minister David Kemp reflects with wry irony that the only issue that unites Australia's thirty-nine public universities is their constant requests to government for more money.[2] For former education policymaker Robert Griew, the overwhelming focus on money in the performance and expectations of universities is an obstacle to a broader and more productive conversation about higher education.[3] But money forms a central strand in the tension between Australia's universities and the society they serve. Any consideration of the place of universities in Australian life must begin by following the money. It is the medium through which Australia's growing demand for higher education confronts the limits to its willingness to pay for it.

Follow the Money

Reflecting on a recent history of Australia's universities, Andrew Norton points out that 'financial shortfalls and funding crises are a regular feature of university life' stretching back well over a century.[4] Australia's universities have long been hostage to the expanding ambitions of society for its higher education institutions and the fluctuations in governments' willingness or capacity to pay for these ambitions. John Dawkins diagnoses the cause of the recurring shortfalls in universities' finances in the ever-expanding demand and cost of higher education and the political and policy limits on governments' ability to pay for those costs.[5] It is important to understand both the demand and the supply side of this dysfunctional equation – why university costs are always rising, and why governments from both sides of politics have been reluctant to commit to fully covering these costs.

The sector's peak body, Universities Australia, reports that the total operating revenue for Australian universities grew from $18.2 billion in 2004 to $33.2 billion in 2018, an 82 per cent increase in the space of just fourteen years.[6] The growth of university budgets is particularly pronounced among the nation's larger higher education institutions. Australia's largest university, Monash University, reported an annual budget of $710 million in 2001; this had grown to $3.1 billion twenty years later.[7] Because they are not-for-profit institutions, the expansion of university budgets shows both an increase in university costs and a growth in revenue. There are several reasons for the remarkable growth in costs over time. The most obvious is the expansion of the number of students they are teaching. In 2001 there were 842,183 students in Australia's higher education sector; by 2020 that number had risen to 1,622,867, an increase of 92 per cent.[8] This growth in demand is not a recent phenomenon: in the twenty years leading up to the millennium, the number of students taking higher degrees had more than doubled. The bulk of these students entered Australia's thirty-nine public universities, the number of which has barely grown since the early 1990s. In other words, the same number of universities has absorbed a 190 per cent growth in the number of students in the three decades since the most recent creation of a new public university. And the numbers keep increasing. Australia is currently experiencing the 'Costello baby boom', where people born during the early 2000s – when then treasurer Peter Costello encouraged

Australian families to have more children – are now reaching university age. According to one estimate, this means that there will be 20 per cent more 18-year-olds in 2029 than there were in 2019 in Victoria and Western Australia.[9] More students must be taught by more academics, accommodated in larger lecture theatres and more tutorial rooms, and serviced by new systems of administration and information resources. Herein lies the most obvious reason for the rise in costs of universities.

There is another reason for the expanding costs of Australia's universities that should be obvious but isn't. Higher education in Australia is an inherently inflationary activity. Australia's universities follow a common model, seeking as comprehensive as possible a coverage of the fields of human knowledge, combining teaching and research, and offering campus-based commuter as opposed to residential education.[10] This formula, seen in Australia as integral to the nature of the public university, contains elements that are increasingly expensive to maintain. The core business of the university is the creation, curation and sharing of knowledge. Australia's universities are required to conduct research to be accredited as universities. The existence of strong research missions in Australia's universities contributes to the global expansion of the stock of human knowledge; indeed, the research enterprise is built around the critique or extension of previous knowledge. Whereas in 1965 one-fifth of Australia's academics described themselves as teaching-only, today that figure is just 3.5 per cent.[11] And the number of research-only academics continues to grow. Few academics would claim that the current state of knowledge in their field has not shifted substantially from the time they were an undergraduate student; for most, today's knowledge in their discipline would be unrecognisable to the academics who taught them. As knowledge expands it becomes more expensive to curate, create and teach. Disciplines subdivide and specialise as a way of understanding and advancing knowledge. Branches of the sciences and engineering have multiplied with the expansion and subdivision of knowledge, each requiring specialist academics, technicians and sometimes administrators to maintain them. Libraries need to stock a growing avalanche of journals, books and databases. Increasingly, specialised research infrastructure is needed as the frontiers of genuinely new discoveries are pushed back. In a range of fields, these genuinely new discoveries rely on increasingly sophisticated – and expensive – equipment. Maintaining comprehensive, research-intensive universities is an exercise in accelerating costs.

The way prestige is measured in universities is another driver of growing costs. As one close study of the Australian higher education sector describes it, 'Since most [academics] teach, and many [academics] perform public service, but fewer win competitive research funds from government or industry, research is the activity that differentiates among and within universities.'[12] In an academic world obsessed by rankings, both inputs and outputs are used to measure and compare research. While the number of publications and citations are the outputs most commonly counted, inputs are measured by the amount of research money won or raised to support the project. When research success is measured by the total quantum of research dollars raised, the incentive is to prioritise more expensive research areas, and to maximise the amount of research funding being sought. With a fixed pot of competitive research funding available, the more a particular university or academic wins, the less is available for competitors.

The recent rise of global rankings has generated intense competition among universities to improve their positions at the expense of rivals. While reviled by many academics, rankings are more and more influential in shaping student choices of where to study, employers' perceptions of the prestige and quality of qualifications, and academics' preferences for where to visit and work.[13] Different rankings are comprised of slightly different measures, but most focus on factors such as research quantum and quality, reputation, academic-to-student ratios, proportion of international students and staff, and teaching and research income. Needless to say, rankings are closely correlated to the wealth of universities. Money helps drive research productivity, buys better facilities and equipment, allows more careful curation of the student mix, and affords a larger number of academics for a given student cohort size. The pervasive attention to the global rankings, and their consequences for universities, means attracting, raising and making money is an increasingly important element of university business: 'It is often remarked that status is more important to universities than money ... For universities, money is a mechanism for securing prestige.'[14] In the words of one close observer,

> Higher education systems are characterised by a reputation race. In this race, higher education institutions are constantly trying to create the best possible images of themselves as highly regarded universities. And this race is expensive.

Higher education institutions will spend all the resources they can find to try to capture an attractive position in the race.[15]

Another specialist argues that the university 'is driven ... to acquire public and private resources for the research, infrastructure, teaching programs and services that underpin status. And the twin objectives, status and resources (quality and quantity) – which tend to produce each other – explain the [university's] accumulative logic and hunger in quasi-markets.'[16]

The incentives to raise money are common to both universities and individual academics. A typical academic grumble heard on campuses across Australia is that an increasing amount of their time is taken up with what they see as distractions from core academic work. Given that research is central to systems of prestige, promotion and job security, most academics are particularly jealous of their research time. Many academics see themselves in competition with their peers and are anxious to maximise their research performance vis-a-vis colleagues who may become more successful, better credentialled or more famous than them. In this context, administrative processes, representational duties and, for some, teaching are viewed as distractions from their ability to conduct research. Money, in the form of competitive research grants or industry partnerships, is a convenient way to dodge these distractions. A major grant or fellowship from the Australian Research Council or the National Health and Medical Research Council often is an excuse for exempting an academic from committees, enables the hiring of research assistants who can pick up administrative tasks, and can include funding to hire another academic to cover the researcher's teaching obligations. Such incentives have given rise to what one study has called a system of 'academic capitalism' in which 'university employees are employed simultaneously by the public sector and are increasingly autonomous from it. They are academics who act as capitalists from within the public sector; they are state-subsidised entrepreneurs'.[17]

The incentivisation of research and pursuit of research funding is linked to the growth in student numbers, producing a reinforcing cycle. Government research grants are not funded to cover the full cost of research, therefore universities have to cover the shortfall from other funding sources. The more successful universities are in winning competitive research funding, the larger the gap they have to fill to cover the full costs of research. The most fungible source of funding is tuition revenue, meaning that as a university becomes more successful in attracting competitive research funding, it needs to recruit more students whose fees will help fund a widening research funding shortfall.[18] All of these various pressures combine to make Australia's universities more expensive by the year. As Andrew Norton points out, as not-for-profit institutions, universities are obliged to spend all of the money they earn on their own operations, perpetually creating higher cost bases that then become vulnerable to sudden downturns in revenue.[19] Howard Bowen identified a tendency for universities to raise all the money they can and spend it on an unlimited list of projects intended to enhance prestige.[20] Australia is fortunate to have such competitive, knowledge-creating institutions – but that doesn't mean it is a society that is prepared to pay for them in full.

The Bucks Stop Here

Until the 1960s, Australia's universities were financed by a combination of government grants and fees paid by students. Beginning with the Menzies government's imperative to expand higher education in Australia, and accelerated by the Whitlam government's pledge to make university education free, public funding of universities increased both in absolute terms and as a proportion of university budgets. Whereas student fees comprised 31.9 per cent of university budgets in 1939, by 1971 they had fallen to 10.4 per cent of the total.[21] Public funding for universities expanded rapidly in the 1970s, doubling between the 1972/73 financial year and 1975/76, and becoming the fastest growing sector of public expenditure – from 4.4 per cent to 8.5 per cent of Commonwealth outlays – during the Whitlam government.[22] Simon Marginson reports that during the 1960s and 1970s there was a reinforcing cycle between individual ambition and desire for social mobility through university education and society's expectations of knowledge-driven growth, which made public attitudes optimistic about funding higher education. This was to run headlong into the austere logic of the 1970s economic recession and later the twin pressures of monetarist economics and globalisation on government budgets. By the end of the 1970s, it was clear that Australian governments 'had lost control of the fiscal politics of higher education'.[23]

But simply turning off the fiscal tap would not solve the problem of expanding higher education outlays. Australians' aspirations for university qualifications had been rising for a generation, as had high school retention rates. After the Fraser government imposed tight limits on higher education funding it became clear that each year a significant number – between 10,000 and 20,000 – of Australians who were qualified to attend university had missed out on a place.[24] The problem of 'unmet demand' for university places started to become politically salient, particularly as it became clear that the shortage of university places was leading to growing competition for access, which meant it was most often students of lower socioeconomic status from outer metropolitan and rural areas who were missing out.[25] The policy platform that Bob Hawke's Australian Labor Party took to the 1983 federal election included a pledge to increase enrolments in Australia's universities and Colleges of Advanced Education (CAE) by 25,000 by 1990.[26] This seemed like an impressive increase, but it would still result in significant unmet demand based on the trends of that time. The ALP won the 1983 election, and as incoming finance minister John Dawkins could see that the government faced a twin challenge: the more open, dynamic economy that treasurer Paul Keating was moving towards would require greater access to higher education for the labour force of the future; but that public funding alone could not finance the expansion of access required.[27] Dawkins had come to believe that without reintroducing student fees, the government was never going to solve the problem of unmet demand, but he faced formidable opposition from colleagues attached to Whitlam's talismanic commitment to free higher education.[28] His successor as finance minister, Peter Walsh, developed a proposal for up-front fees and means-tested loans which failed to get caucus endorsement.[29]

In 1984, Dawkins moved to the trade portfolio in the second Hawke ministry, from where he made the first of two enduring changes to higher education funding in Australia. Two separate independent reports – one commissioned by the immigration minister, the other by the foreign minister – had considered the future of international students in Australia. The Goldring review into private overseas education in Australia recommended that government closely regulate numbers of international students, the English language standards required and the fees charged. The Jackson review into Australia's aid program recommended the clear separation of aid-based and full-fee international education and supported permitting universities to recruit international students and keep the fees.[30] Dawkins could see the closure of sectors of the economy that was unfolding as a result of deregulation and tariff reductions, and believed higher education could emerge as a new export sector. He sent a trade delegation to Asia with instructions to gauge the potential for growth for Australia's international higher education sector, and was pleased when the delegation reported strong potential to develop education as an export industry.[31] Dawkins took a proposal to Cabinet arguing that Australia's universities be permitted to recruit international students and retain the fees, provided that the amount charged was sufficient to ensure there was no cross-subsidisation of educating international students by the Australian taxpayer, and that the problem of unmet demand was addressed to ensure that international students could not be accused of taking places from Australians. The proposal was opposed by the education and immigration departments, as well as law enforcement, but carried the day on the promise to create, in the words of the Jackson Report, 'an export industry in which institutions are encouraged to compete for students and funds.'[32] From 1986, Australia's universities could freely recruit international students under a policy framework that established an 'institution-driven, lightly regulated market' allowing universities to set prices and keep the income.[33] It quickly grew into a major source of revenue, as well as an unstated excuse for governments to back away from a funding framework that would expand higher education access for Australians with taxpayers' money.

In 1987 Dawkins became Minister for Employment, Education and Training in the third Hawke government, and would go on to drive the second major change in higher education funding. His ideas on higher education were well-developed due to his time as shadow education minister prior to the 1983 election, where he devised Labor's education policy. As the minister responsible for employment, Dawkins was acutely aware that the government's economic reform agenda would have extensive economic and social impacts, and that the higher education sector would need to prepare Australians for the jobs of the future.[34] He also realised that public funding alone would not address the unmet demand problem. A 1986 report into higher education showed that real government spending on higher education had flatlined for a decade, while student numbers had increased by 25 per cent over the same period.[35] Dawkins' Green Paper, released at the end of 1987, predicted a greater than 40 per cent increase in demand for higher education by the end of the century – an expansion that was estimated to cost an extra $1 billion over that period.[36] However, he faced strong opposition within caucus to the reintroduction of fees from those who saw free tertiary education as a lasting monument to Whitlam and an essential measure in breaking the nexus between social privilege and higher education. As trade minister, Dawkins had persuaded his colleagues on the Expenditure Review Committee to require universities and CAEs to collect a $250 Higher Education Administration Charge from each student. Opposed by then education minister Susan Ryan, the HEAC both avoided confronting the ALP shibboleth of no tuition fees while at the same time opening the door to student contributions to the cost of their education.[37] Concurrent with the release of the Green Paper, Dawkins commissioned former premier of New South Wales Neville Wran to conduct a review of higher education funding 'to develop options for supplementing the funding of the Australian higher education system which could involve contributions from students, their parents and employers'.[38] The Wran Report, noting that university graduates recouped a higher financial return during their working lives, recommended that all students be charged approximately 20 per cent of the costs of their courses, to be deferred and paid back to the government through the tax system once graduates' income had passed a particular threshold.[39] ANU economist Bruce Chapman was commissioned to create options for how such a user-pays system could work, and in 1988 the Higher Education Contribution Scheme (HECS) was born.[40] It was an ingenious and path-breaking policy innovation. Students would be charged for part of their education via a deferred loans scheme to be repaid only once they had reached a certain level of prosperity. Higher education had been made accessible to people from all socioeconomic classes, but the cost to the taxpayer had been defrayed onto the beneficiaries of university education. Equity and partial privatisation came together. The system has remained in place ever since, with subsequent governments adjusting upwards the amount of course costs contributed by students and downwards the income thresholds at which repayments commence.

The other element of the Dawkins reforms that would have significant implications for the cost and financing of higher education was the creation of a 'Unified National System' of universities that would be expected to teach and research, and which would be funded and evaluated by the Commonwealth government according to common rubrics. This brought to an end Australia's binary system of higher education, which had separated higher education into a university sector and a system of CAEs. The binary system was the result of the 1964 Martin Report on higher education in Australia, which sought to square the circle of rising numbers of people accessing higher education at an acceptable cost.[41] In accepting the report's recommendations, the Menzies government agreed to fund universities for teaching and research but to fund CAEs for teaching only. Both types of tertiary institution would confer bachelor's degrees, but only universities would be funded to conduct research and train doctoral students. The CAEs were expected to specialise in technical and vocational training, while universities were expected to confine themselves to scholarship and disciplinary specialisation; indeed, the Martin Report expressed alarm at the drift towards technological and vocational interests in Australia's universities.[42] The CAEs were a popular choice for students, particularly those from working-class backgrounds and who chose to study part-time. They significantly reduced pressures on universities to train undergraduate students, and within a decade of the Martin Report a majority of undergraduates were enrolled in CAEs.[43] The Dawkins reforms, which specified a minimum size for any institution wanting recognition as a university and offering research money only to universities conducting research, spurred CAEs to merge to form universities or to merge with universities – thereby baking mass universities into Australia's higher education system. From then on, Australia would only have universities, which would be required to teach, research and conduct doctoral training – with significant implications for the cost of higher education in Australia.

The changes driven by John Dawkins in the 1980s have recast the picture on university financing. The contribution of international student fees and deferred domestic student fees supported by income-contingent loans to the expansion of Australian universities has assumed proportions that are now critical to the viability of the higher education sector. With direct Commonwealth grants to universities stagnating in real terms, international and HECS fees are assuming an ever-greater role in supporting university teaching and research. Andrew Norton observes that until COVID hit, revenue from overseas students was set to exceed Commonwealth grants to universities; in the aftermath of the pandemic, he predicts that domestic student fees (now rebranded as the Higher Education Loan Program, or HELP) will become the largest contributor to higher education funding.[44] Surveying his achievements as minister in 1988, Dawkins joked that the Australian economy might one day ride on the mortarboard.[45] His dream of the development of a major services export sector has become a reality, with higher education Australia's largest non-commodity export, earning over \$6 billion a year. This should be a matter to celebrate, but it is rare to hear anyone speaking positively about the international entrepreneurialism of our universities outside of the academy. Indeed, the commercial acumen of Australia's universities has become a major target for criticism – this tells us much about the role many think universities should play in Australian life.

Resolutely Public

Unlike in Britain or the United States, Australia's universities from inception were conceived by governments and directed to serve state and society.[46] William Charles Wentworth – the prime mover in the founding of Australia's first university in Sydney in 1850 – argued that as the colony of New South Wales shifted towards self-government it needed a university-educated class, and without a local university 'the native youth of the country could not now obtain the education which would fit them for high offices in the state'.[47] This began a tradition of the founding of universities in each colony or state by an act of the local parliament and accountable to the state parliament – Sydney (1850), Melbourne (1853), Adelaide (1874), Tasmania (1890), Queensland (1909) and Western Australia (1911). The federal government joined in, establishing its own Australian National University in Canberra in 1946. This began a second wave of founding new universities in the postwar years, again by acts of state parliaments. The third wave of university creation, which was sparked by the Dawkins reforms and creation of the unified national system after 1988, involved the amalgamation of universities and various non-university tertiary institutions – each requiring the assent of the government of the state or territory it was based in.

For the first century following 1850, Australia's six original universities were funded primarily by annual state government grants, supplemented by lecture and examination fees and gifts from donors.[48] But by the early 1950s these sources of funding were patently inadequate, prompting the Australian Vice-chancellors' Committee to issue a report titled 'A Crisis in the Finances and Development of Australia's Universities' in 1952.[49] Prime Minister Robert Menzies, who had previously mused about a role for the federal government in education, commissioned Sir Keith Murray, chairman of the British Universities Grants Committee, to head a review of Australia's universities. The Murray Report of November 1957 sketched out a big-picture vision of a substantial role to be played by Australia's universities in the development of the nation, bolstering liberal social values as well as providing the knowledge and professional training for an advanced economy.[50] Menzies accepted the report and its recommendations promptly; in tabling the report personally in parliament he said

The social, scientific, economic and industrial complexities of Australia today are largely beyond the imagination of forty years ago. Great skill achieved after high training is no longer to be regarded as something to be admired in a few. We must, on a broad basis, become a more and more educated democracy if we are to raise our spiritual, intellectual and material living standards. Viewed in this way our universities are to be regarded not as a home of privilege for a few but as something essential to the lives of millions of people who may never enter their doors.[51]

By determining universities as central to Australia's future, Menzies established the rationale for the Commonwealth government to assume greater responsibility for funding the universities through a newly created University Grants Committee. In committing taxpayers' money to an expanding university sector, Menzies was careful to stress the contract between those going to university and the public good: '[university students] will, I am sure, not forget that … the community is accepting heavy burdens in order that, through the training of university graduates, the community may be served.'[52]

Higher education became central to the ethos of the postwar economic boom, 'expected to contribute to economic growth and development, to the broadening of the character and reach of modern citizenship, to rising living standards and quality of life, to widening opportunities, to greater equality and social reform, and to a growing number of individual futures'.[53] In a growing economy in which the number of professional jobs was expanding rapidly, wage income was at historically high levels compared to inherited income, and immigration and full employment were boosting public finances, governments from Menzies to Whitlam were comfortable with both stimulating demand for higher education and funding the expansion of universities and university places.[54] This virtuous cycle collapsed during the 1970s recession: as unemployment rose and the number of professional jobs shrank, continuing high levels of university education delivered growing queues of university graduates who could not find employment appropriate to their qualifications.[55] As the economic gloom of the stagflation era deepened, a new neoliberal critique of public funding of higher education gained momentum. Critics such as the godfather of monetarist economics, Milton Friedman, argued that contrary to Menzies' belief, the benefits of higher education were confined to the individual's increased earning capacity, and therefore university students, not taxpayers, should fund higher education.[56] Public funding, critics argued, was regressive, taxing all in society to the further benefit of a privileged few; in the words of Opposition leader Malcolm Fraser, free university meant a 'wharf labourer paying taxes to subsidise a lawyer's education.'[57] Furthermore, critics claimed that public subsidisation and the expansion of access to tertiary education had caused students to devalue the opportunity of being at university, leading to a sharp decline in quality and standards. The solution was to subject higher education to market forces, encouraging competition among universities based on quality and allowing students the freedom to choose among the universities on quality and price. It was a solution that would have far-reaching and complex consequences for Australia's universities.

The Liberal–National Coalition won government in 1996, inheriting, among other things, a higher education system reshaped by the Dawkins reforms. In January 1997, education minister Amanda Vanstone commissioned Roderick West, former headmaster of Trinity Grammar School in Sydney, to review the state of Australia's higher education sector and its effectiveness in meeting the nation's social, economic, scientific and cultural needs over the next two decades. The West Report, presented to Vanstone's successor, Dr David Kemp, applauded the system's expansion of access to higher education, its innovation in deferred student loans and its encouragement of entrepreneurialism in international education, but was critical of the system's centralised planning, controls on tuition charges and centralised regulation of student places and funding. According to the report, the system inhibited flexibility, innovation and differentiation and skewed incentives away from excellence in teaching towards research, while removing the incentives to minimise costs.[58] The report resonated with Kemp's own ideas. A former academic, he had written the higher education policy for the 'Fightback!' platform that the Liberal Party had taken to the 1993 federal election. It had been critical of the heavy regulation of the Dawkins system, which it argued produced 'barriers to efficiency and adaptation to the needs of the market' and led to unmet demand of 30,000 Australians excluded from higher education by government-imposed quotas.[59] Having received the West report, Kemp prepared a Cabinet submission proposing to deregulate the number of places universities could offer and what they could charge, and allow students greater choice over where to study, while providing student loans, a universal tuition subsidy and a loans scheme repayable through the tax system.[60] The submission was leaked to the Opposition and ruled out by Cabinet following a storm of protest and a scare campaign raising the prospect of spiralling university fees and student debt. Kemp's attempt to introduce further market forces into the Australian university sector had failed, as did attempts by his Liberal education minister successors Brendan Nelson and Christopher Pyne. Australia, it seemed, wanted its universities to remain resolutely public and regulated by government.

When Labor returned to power after the 2007 election, it arrived with a big education agenda driven by deputy prime minister and education minister Julia Gillard. Gillard commissioned former vice-chancellor of the University of South Australia Denise Bradley to conduct a review of the Australian higher education sector. The Bradley Report outlined an imperative to increase levels of tertiary education in Australia as critical to maintaining Australia's economic success, recommending that all qualified students should have access to and choice of university, and that universities should be free to enrol as many students as they wished and be funded for those places.[61] From 2008 to 2010, the government increased caps on student places, and from 2012 deregulated them altogether, ushering in a six-year experiment known as 'the demand-driven system'. Between 2008 and 2018 undergraduate student numbers increased by 36 per cent, with three universities more than doubling their enrolments. The highest growth rates were in health, science, engineering and information technology.

The Coalition – which returned to power in 2013 determined to rein in spending – and the education minister, Christopher Pyne, commissioned a review of the demand-driven system. The review recommended the continuation of the system, with some modifications, such as extending it to sub-bachelor's degrees and non-university higher education providers.[62] The government accepted this advice, while trying to restrain the cost by reducing the government contribution per student place. Failing to convince the Senate to support this, the government instituted a cap on the total grant to each university at 2017 levels with no adjustment for inflation, no funding for enrolment growth and only the possibility of indexation for population growth based on performance.[63] In 2020, the government legislated a major reform, known as 'Job-ready Graduates', continuing to specify its contribution towards student places while dramatically changing the prices charged for degrees, making them significantly cheaper for skills deemed in demand and more expensive for those deemed less economically necessary. Universities are free to determine how they will allocate government-supported places, but within a cap of the total government grant. The experiment with demand-driven funding had hit the cold reality of how much Australia was prepared to pay for its higher education needs. Regulation had returned.

Poor Little Rich Unis

Kemp reflects that any institution that relies on public funding will be underfunded, because governments are always under pressure to deliver new initiatives, leaving existing commitments to be funded according to their political salience.[64] For most of the history of universities in Australia, the financial requirements of higher education have outstripped governments' willingness to pay. Former finance minister Lindsay Tanner reflects ruefully that higher education is generally seen by politicians as a second-order political issue, which no doubt explains the stagnating rate of public funding for Australia's universities.[65] Repeated attempts by university leaders to stimulate greater government spending on the sector have relied on a range of strategies. One is alarm, claiming that the miserly spending on higher education will damage the sector, leading to national decline. Another is aspirational, pointing out the benefits that universities bring to Australia and promising more if greater public investment is forthcoming. A third is to benchmark Australia's higher education funding against those of other advanced economies, implying that Australia will fail to keep up if rates of investment in universities don't rise.

These tactics have failed to work. Australian governments and publics by and large seem unconvinced that greater funding for universities justifies taking money from other programs. The repeated appeals for more government funding have led to the impression that Australia's universities are habitual mendicants on the public purse, an impression that sits ill with the much-publicised images of architectural grandeur, lush gardens and gleaming equipment in their publicity campaigns. Every year, at annual report time, university surpluses and vice-chancellors' salaries gain great attention and are often juxtaposed against their requests for more money. Stories of impending decline sit incongruously beside the trumpeting of the world-class quality of those same universities. Australia seems to want its universities to be public institutions but is unconvinced of their need for more money. The compromise is the growing proportion of student loans and international fees in the financing of ostensibly public institutions.

Selling Out?

Australia's universities are a strange hybrid: part tightly regulated, underfunded public institutions; part highly entrepreneurial, innovative education exporters. Herein lies the contradiction: universities seem to be rich and successful but are always complaining about being underfunded. As the level of public funding stagnates and revenue from domestic students is capped, universities have been forced to teach more students with less money per student. Class sizes have increased, facilities have become more crowded and the student experience has been compromised. Rates of academic casualisation have grown. International student fees have filled what would otherwise have become unsustainable shortfalls in infrastructure, research capability and student equity programs. Realising that international education is an increasingly competitive prestige market, universities have invested the bulk of those fees in attributes that build prestige: research performance, sparkling new facilities, slick marketing campaigns.

Inevitably the incongruity produces outrage. Critics, from both the left and the right, argue that the pursuit of money has perverted the basic idea of the university. Academic rigour, they claim, has been compromised by the need to attract and retain students. The freedom to think big thoughts has been crushed by the neoliberal logic of chasing research funding and seeking commercialisation opportunities. Australia's universities have been compared to banks, where a culture based on growth and profits has undermined a commitment to customers and the public interest.[66] The sarcasm is not far behind. Universities are 'rapacious corporations', chasing international student fees to further staff already bloated bureaucracies, or so that vice-chancellors can build 'Taj Mahals' to themselves.[67] Large surpluses, such as those recorded by Sydney, Monash and Melbourne in 2022, and vice-chancellors' salaries, are contrasted to the underpayment of casual workers, staff layoffs during the COVID years and stories of poor student experience and student poverty.

As Australia's universities contemplated the prospect of severe financial losses thanks to the closure of Australia's borders during the pandemic, the chorus of schadenfreude became constant. Here were the consequences of universities' 'broken business models', the result of self-seeking university leaders imperilling these public institutions by making them overly dependent on one source of revenue. The crisis, argued two professors from Macquarie Business School, decisively demonstrated that vice-chancellors were not worth their huge salaries.[68] Universities had become 'addicted' to international student fees, and the sharp reduction in these was the intervention the country needed, forcing the rapacious corporations to return to their core business. The government was urged not to intervene to support the universities because this would remove the incentive for them to reform. Presumably 'reformed' universities would have no international students, less funding for research, little capability to maintain or add to facilities and even worse staff–student rations.

Such anger and contempt towards Australia's universities flows like a current through society, never far from the surface, easily provoked by an anecdote or caustic remark. It is acknowledged within the universities with a sense of bemusement. Why don't Australians admire the success of their universities as they celebrate the successes of their sporting teams, filmmakers, musicians and actors? Why is their entrepreneurialism in earning significant revenue in a global market not appreciated in the same way that the commercial successes of Australia's mining corporations or investment banks are? Why was the closure of Australia's borders a reckoning for universities' 'broken business models' but a national concern for the tourism industry?

The choices, tensions, compromises and passions surrounding university financing in Australia reveal an important facet of this society's ambivalence towards them. A growing number of Australians want to attend university and they want their children to do so. They are comfortable with the government regulating how much they will have to pay to do so, and with no real increase in what the government pays the universities. But they are not comfortable with the entrepreneurial side universities have revealed in the one area where they are not heavily regulated – the market for international students. Universities' investment in prestige and building of corporate capabilities tears at the sublime ideal of the university by raising a deep cultural antagonism between money and authenticity. Reaching back to the Stoic philosophers and the Christian embrace of poverty, there is a moral assumption in Australian society that wealth is a distraction from authenticity and perfection. Western universities emerged from medieval monastic orders, most of which had taken vows of poverty and rejection of private property to better focus on attaining spiritual purity. The Reformation emerged from a spreading disgust that the church had abandoned its poverty in the pursuit of wealth and glory. Similar undertones can be heard in the anger at Australian universities' entrepreneurialism and commercial success.

This is a faux conversation, driven by partial understandings and emotionalism rather than rationality. While discussions of funding should never be the sole shaper of higher education policy, they do need to be an integral part of a broader public consensus on the role of higher education in modern Australia. The problem is that considerations of money have been allowed to lead and mould higher education policy rather than to follow a bigger conversation and consensus about the role of universities in Australian life. Higher education policy should also rethink whether the declining public share of funding for the sector is ultimately in Australia's interests. As Thomas Piketty speculates, 'the stagnation of [public] educational investment in the rich countries since the 1980s may help to explain not only the rise of inequality but also the slowing of economic growth.'[69] Yet the public discussion between universities and governments over funding has become stale, a dialogue of mutual incomprehension. The first year of the pandemic revealed this. As universities faced looming financial crises from campus lockdowns and closed borders, education minister Dan Tehan delivered $1 billion to support university research and an additional $550 million for short courses and other concessions, yet the sector largely pocketed the extra money and continued complaining about being locked out of JobKeeper.[70] A much larger national conversation on the real costs and benefits of higher education in Australia needs to take place. Without substantial rethinking and re-engineering – a shared task for universities, governments and broader society – the place of universities in Australian life will become ever more fraught and dysfunctional.

2

Value

NOTHING EVOKED THE crisis that COVID posed to Australia's universities more powerfully than the pictures of empty campuses that circulated on traditional and social media in those first terrible weeks and months after March 2020. Avenues, quads and lawns that weeks before had hummed with people fell quiet – untouched by human footfall; undisturbed by laughter, conversation and music; uncluttered by stalls, queues and tours.

The gathering of community and the pooling of potential, interest and curiosity has animated universities for centuries. Since they first sprang up, in different locations and cultures, these centres of knowledge have acted as magnets – agglomerations of talent, ambition, learning and inquiry. The Universities of Bologna and Paris, established almost a thousand years ago, were communities of students and scholars, gathered into 'nations', reflecting their attractive pull across borders. They were also self-governing communities: the University of Bologna owed its existence to Holy Roman emperor

Frederick Barbarossa, who issued a decree exempting the university from temporal laws. These institutions adopted the Latin title *universitas* rather than the more commonly used *studium generale*; it is a significant choice, indicating that they wanted to be known by their governance arrangements as self-determining corporations rather than by what they did. Inherent in this terminology was the assertion that authority within the corporate body rested with its individual members; in the words of Larry Siedentop, 'authority flows upwards rather than from the top down',[1] establishing a clear norm of collegial governance of universities by their academic communities. So much of the history of universities in the Western world consists of tensions between self-governing universities and their country's government. More recently, however, the tensions have migrated onto campus. Protests have seen students and academics besiege chancelleries, sometimes occupying offices and defenestrating the contents of vice-chancellors' filing cabinets. The communities of students and scholars, it would seem, are fracturing. Some of those most disillusioned with Australia's universities are those who work and study in them.

A common charge among academics and students alike is that Australia's universities have become too corporatised, that they are more interested in budgets, strategic initiatives and image than in knowledge, argument and pedagogy. Historian Hannah Forsyth writes of a 'Deputy Vice-chancellor epidemic' as university chancelleries become filled with managers who are divorced from the academic work of the university but spend their time and the university's resources administering it as a business enterprise.[2] Academics complain that they are increasingly tied up with trivial administrative tasks – completing training modules, conducting student surveys, submitting lists of publications and activities – even while the number of non-academic administrators increases around them. Many note that the salaries of vice-chancellors and their executives continue to rise, while academics at the chalk-face are squeezed for resources and ever more reliant on academic support staff on precarious casual contracts. Across Australia's universities there is a pervasive sense of powerlessness against this rising tide of corporatism. Old systems of academic collegiality and collective decision-making still exist in living memory, but appear to have been swept aside by a ruthless business culture and a command-and-control framework of hierarchy and initiative. Simon Marginson and Mark Considine have carefully documented and examined the emergence of what they call the 'enterprise university' in Australia.[3] University communities are large, comprising tens of thousands of students and thousands of staff, and extend out to their families and friendship groups. Before long, this disgruntlement about how universities are run starts to become widespread throughout a large slice of Australian life. Herein lies another angle on Australians' ambivalence about their universities.

The direction of university governance in Australia is driven by a never-resolved uncertainty about the value of our universities. When they were first founded, the value was clear: each year they would produce a stream of professionals – doctors, lawyers, officials, dentists, diplomats – who were needed to address obvious social needs. Universities' value to society was confirmed by the professional associations that accredited them to train the next generations of the critical knowledge workers of the day.[4] Three trends combined in the 1970s and 1980s to confound this certainty about the value of universities. One was the proliferation of professional training being offered by universities. Occupations that had formerly been learned on the job, such as nursing or teaching, started to require a university qualification. University enrolments steepled upwards, as did the bewildering array of qualifications they offered. Questions arose as to whether a fancy university degree was really necessary, and about whether university training really was superior to on-the-job skilling that had worked previously.

A second trend was the promise of social mobility for the children of families that had never attended university, creating escalating demand for university places which the sector could not meet. The third trend was the assumption of responsibility for financing universities and this expansion of enrolments by the federal government. The difference between state and federal government funding is that the latter is more immediately salient to taxpayers, and the trade-offs – what is not being funded because of university financing – are more obvious. The more the federal government is on the hook for financing Australia's universities, the more persistent the questions about what value society gets for this largesse towards universities. As Australia's universities grew and became talked about as increasingly more central to the country's future, anxiety about the quality of their contribution to the country mounted. The call for greater accountability from these effete, opaque institutions became more insistent. And to provide reassurance about their value, Australia's universities needed to change.

Et in Arcadia Ego

Tabling the Murray Report in parliament in 1957, Prime Minister Robert Menzies remarked that 'a university may look to governments, and perhaps primarily to governments, for land and buildings and equipment. But its ultimate achievement will depend, as ever, upon the zeal and quality of its staff and those who train under them.'[5] Here was a statement encapsulating government's relationship to universities that was prevalent at the time: while the state could support academic institutions, it was not competent to judge the value of what they did; but it trusted universities to ensure that they employed the best academics and students who would conduct academic work to the best of their abilities. It had been a longstanding claim that academic work could only be judged by academics because governments, churches or other authorities in society were not competent nor trusted to appraise it. Universities must therefore be self-governing institutions.[6] This doctrine had been asserted forcefully by America's leading universities in the early twentieth century and became foundational to modern notions of academic freedom.[7] Self-government and peer governance were principles that applied to the university as a whole but also permeated the entire enterprise: as specialists in particular disciplines, individual academics' work could only be assessed, critiqued and verified by other academics with the appropriate levels of disciplinary expertise. In common with the professions, academic expertise implied local occupational authority as an alternative to the management hierarchies that governed other institutions: government agencies, private companies, the military, schools.[8]

These considerations had particular implications for university governance and relations with the state. The original form of university governance was academic collegiality and highly consensual decision-making. Academic leaders, such as vice-chancellors and deans, were elected by the academic community, from the academic community. These were short-term, part-time roles, rarely accompanied by additional remuneration or prestige, but undertaken out of a sense of service to the institution and the profession. These traditions live on in the institution of the academic board at many Australian universities, even if many of the boards have not kept pace with the representativeness of other institutions in society. As Australia's universities grew in size and complexity in the late nineteenth century, suggestions were made that they needed permanent, full-time 'chief executive officers' to oversee the operations of the entire institution. A royal commission into the University of Melbourne rejected such a proposal in 1904; in 1916, the university advocated for the creation of the position of 'principal' to play such a role. The university council accepted the recommendation but never funded the position.[9] It was only in 1926 that the University of Sydney appointed the first vice-chancellor in Australia, with the other universities following some years afterwards. However, while the new vice-chancellors were remunerated and full-time positions, the tradition was still to elect them from within the academy. Unsurprisingly, these archaic titles and rituals of representation made universities utterly mystifying to those outside them, particularly governments. But there was a clear sense that universities were self-governing institutions because they needed to be to supply society with the expertise that government itself could not furnish. As historian Conrad Russell put it in 1989, 'Universities and the state need each other precisely because their values and priorities are so different from each other. Each depends on the other for those things which its professional discipline and code of values makes it least able to understand.'[10] Reciprocal incomprehension – undoubtedly. Reciprocal need – perhaps. Reciprocal appreciation – not so fast.

Ivory Towers and Sheltered Workshops

In common with other English-speaking countries, Australia has inherited a long tradition of scepticism about academics and universities. 'Academic' is widely used as an antonym for practical, relevant or important, and is often a trigger for derision or dismissal. In the American context, historian Richard Hofstadter describes an attitude of 'resentment and suspicion of the life of the mind and those who are considered to represent it; and a disposition constantly to minimise the value of that life.'[11] He argues that this arises from the sheer incongruity of the intellectual enterprise with the capabilities and attitudes that society values, such as intelligence:

> Intellect ... is the critical, creative, and contemplative side of the mind. Whereas intelligence seeks to grasp, manipulate, re-order, adjust, intellect examines, ponders, wonders, theorises, criticizes, imagines. Intelligence will seize the immediate meaning in a situation and evaluate it. Intellect evaluates evaluations, and looks for the meanings of situations as a whole.[12]

These qualities of the intellect stand opposed to many of the social norms that organise everyday Australian life: pragmatism, achievement, materialism, egalitarianism, common sense. While Australian society has undoubtedly inherited many of these from the utilitarian ethos of nineteenth-century Britain, they have been sharpened by the imperative of building a new society through hard work, which also helped furnish a justification for the dispossession of those deemed not to be 'using' it.

While cerebral institutions and occupations might be tolerated and ignored in good times, they come to be resented when society is doing it tough. As the 1970s recession savaged the Australian economy, critical attention was trained on the institutions associated with the era of Keynesian big-spending government: public utilities, public broadcasting, public hospitals and schools – and universities.[13] Institutions and workers with the security of government funding were regarded with suspicion, suspected of being 'bludgers' while the rest of society struggled. Many came to the view that 'academics are little better than middle-class welfare-scroungers, indulging their hobbies at public expense'.[14] Australia's universities were increasingly derided as 'large-scale workers cooperatives' and 'sheltered workshops for intellectuals', according to one account.[15] In hard times, the apparent privilege of universities, and academics' seeming disengagement from the immediate concerns of society, only heightened antipathies. By the mid-1980s, the Coalition Opposition had established a Waste Watch Committee, determined to find and exploit examples of what it saw as the misuse of public money. It pounced on a list of university research projects approved for funding through the

Australian Research Grants Committee (ARGC), and made much fun of projects such as 'Motherhood in Ancient Rome', 'Syntax in Jane Austen's Novels' and 'Techniques of 17th Century Dutch Shipbuilding'. The uproar on talkback radio led Cabinet to cut the ARGC's funding.[16]

To respond to the recession, the Hawke government developed a policy narrative around the failure of the old Australian economy and the need to construct a new, more flexible, productive and innovative economy. Treasurer Paul Keating told John Laws in 1986, 'if this government cannot get the adjustment, get manufacturing going again and keep moderate wage outcomes and a sensible economic policy then Australia is basically done for. We will just end up being a third-rate economy ... a banana republic.'[17] Shortly after, Hawke pledged his government to 'the great task of national renewal, reconstruction and revitalisation.'[18] With the rest of the Western world in similar difficulties, the booming economies of Asia emerged as the model to follow. Japan, South Korea, Hong Kong and Singapore continued to grow strongly, powered by innovation, manufacturing excellence, flexibility and high levels of productivity. Unless Australia learned from its neighbours, it risked becoming the 'poor white trash of Asia' – a remark attributed to then Singaporean prime minister Lee Kuan Yew. Studies such as the World Bank's 'East Asian Miracle' report identified Asian societies' investments in education as a crucial component in enabling dynamic high-growth economies.[19] When education minister John Dawkins rose in parliament in September 1987 to deliver a ministerial statement on higher education, he said,

The ongoing adjustments required in the structure of our economy will place a much greater premium on technical knowledge and labour force skills, and likewise on quality, innovation and technology. These attributes will also be a vital factor in our productivity performance and in the speed of our adaptation to future changes in economic circumstances ... Our universities and colleges of advanced education are the main source of the highly educated men and women so essential to our continued economic growth. They provide the scientists, engineers and technologists we need to develop and maintain a modern industrial structure.[20]

Universities were being thrust to the forefront of Australia's challenge to reinvent its economy, but faced deep scepticism from government, business and society as to whether they were capable of playing this role; the stereotypical moth-eaten professor seemed utterly inadequate in the gleaming, dynamic economy of the future. The paradox of becoming vital to Australia's economic success was that universities were liable to be blamed for perceived inadequacies in the country's economic performance. Where Australia lags in innovation and commercialisation, the blame is sheeted home to failures in university research and entrepreneurialism, as well as to vocational training and schools. When skills shortages impede business, universities are accused of not educating properly or in the right disciplines or skills. Where a Singapore or an Israel seems to be outpacing Australia in building a high-technology economy, questions are asked about the entrepreneurialism of university academics. As universities are exhorted to become more central to society's success, so society seems less and less satisfied with what universities are contributing. So when Dawkins released a Green Paper on higher education in December 1987, he placed universities at the centre of Australia's response to domestic challenges and global dynamism before declaring:

> Australia must now examine the performance of its higher education system. We must ask the people and companies of Australia, whose taxes provide the resources for higher education, what demands and expectations the country has of its institutions and whether the institutions are responding to those demands and expectations.[21]

Demanding Accountability

By placing higher education at the centre of Australia's economic reinvention, Dawkins sought to justify expanding access and funding to the sector at a time of budget stringency. It was not a good time to be arguing for increased funding to large public sector organisations. The dominance of monetarist theory fostered a belief that every dollar taken from the taxpayer and used by the public sector was one less dollar able to produce value in the private economy. Public institutions needed to show that they were contributing to economic growth, so the minister sought to use his Green Paper to move the conversation away from money and onto the number of graduates needed and produced, and their ultimate benefit to the country.[22] He was clear that more money meant more accountability: universities would need to demonstrate that they were using the money they were receiving to deliver the outcomes that were expected of them. The intent outlined in the Green Paper was 'to promote further growth in the higher education sector in a manner consistent with our economic, social and cultural needs'. The paper signalled that 'the achievement of such growth in a climate of continuing financial restraint will require close attention to the efficient use of resources in higher education and to the institutional arrangements by which those resources are provided'. It then drew a direct correlation between the efficiency of our higher education system, and the strength of economic growth and how easily it could be achieved.[23]

The references to efficient use of resources, efficiency of performance and institutional arrangements would have been familiar to Commonwealth public servants, who were undergoing a process of reforms that Dawkins had instigated when he was finance minister in the first Hawke government. Blocked by Treasurer Paul Keating from pursuing his interest in tax reform, Dawkins was given responsibility for public service reform. Inspired by examples of new public management implemented in other countries, his public service reforms sought to apply private sector management techniques to the Commonwealth bureaucracy.[24] These reforms were in line with the tenor of the times, as large public sector institutions found themselves either on the road to privatisation or under pressure to corporatise their operations.[25] The Green Paper on higher education unsurprisingly had a whole section on university management, stating at the outset, 'structuring management to ensure efficient and effective decision making is central' to the government's reforms in higher education.[26] Those reading the minister's initial thoughts on institutional reform of universities could have no doubt that he endorsed the 1980s valorisation of the private sector as a model of productivity and accountability in organisational governance. The Green Paper sketched a picture of the proliferation of large and cumbrous bureaucracies eating up resources and slowing decision-making in Australia's universities. Marginson and Considine characterised the minister's approach as 'a form of fundamentalism that finds fault with every and any aspect of universities which is different from corporations'.[27] The Green Paper exhorted university governance processes to change to allow 'strong leadership through fostering efficiency, setting priorities, promoting client orientation and undertaking corporate planning and review'.[28]

Despite the obvious reforming zeal, there was a recognition that universities were self-governing communities making it 'not appropriate for [government] to dictate internal management structures'. It was here that the minister revealed to Australia's universities the arms-length techniques of the regulatory state: 'The Government's primary concern is not with the nature of internal management but with the output as reflected in the development and implementation of strategic planning, performance monitoring and review'.[29] The approach to regulation adopted by Dawkins had its philosophical roots in the legal framework of principal–agent relations, which presumes that agents will adopt self-interested strategies with opportunism and guile that diverge from the intentions of their principals. The prescribed solution was clearer hierarchies of power and responsibility, precise goals, devolution of resources and responsibility, rigorous performance measurement and reporting, and transparency to governing boards.[30] The higher education White Paper released by Dawkins in July 1988 stated that 'the quest for quality and efficiency in an era of rapid change will require both innovative policymaking by institutional governing bodies and strong, decisive implementation of those policies by institutional managers.'[31] Specific funding was set aside by the government for the review and reform of university executive structures and for professional training for middle managers, with the warning that 'the Government's restructuring of the higher education system will create an environment that fosters and rewards improved management practices.'[32] Beyond the strong signals that were being sent to universities to corporatise their governance, Dawkins wielded the power of the purse. In order to access the expanded funding being offered, universities had to opt in to the Unified National System, as the Dawkins reforms were officially termed. To do so, they had to commit to improved management decision-making and stronger planning and accountability. Each university entered into a funding agreement with the government, setting out its mission, goals and activities; future funding was contingent on fulfilling the agreed goals.[33]

Under New Management

Predictably, there was a great deal of disquiet among universities that the minister's imposition of corporate management techniques was an intrusion into academic freedom and governance. The White Paper breezily dismissed such concerns:

> The Government's aim is to enhance the autonomy and
> capacity of institutions to direct their resources flexibly and
> effectively to meet their designated goals. It is not, as some
> respondents [to the Green Paper] have suggested, to reduce
> that autonomy nor to limit the opportunities for staff to influ-
> ence institutional decisions.[34]

Gradually, Australia's universities grudgingly joined the Unified National System and accepted its conditions. The only standout was the University of Melbourne, whose vice-chancellor, David Penington, tried to convince his counterpart at the University of Sydney that if the country's two oldest universities refused to join, the reforms would fail. When University of Sydney vice-chancellor John Ward refused Pennington's request, Melbourne became the last university to join. The governance changes to universities required by the Unified National System concentrated on two elements: the role and powers of the vice-chancellor, and the size and duties of governing councils. The higher education White Paper spent some time on university governing councils, criticising them for their excessive size and the orientation of their members. It advocated for smaller councils and stressed that they should emphasise the 'trustee' aspects of their mandates: 'that is, on setting broad directions and policies for the institution, and on the consideration of regular reports and reviews of how well the institution is performing.'[35] While the White Paper made no specific recommendations on the expertise or backgrounds of university council members, the strong corporate tenor of the Dawkins reforms resulted in the increasing recruitment of people with business and corporate backgrounds to these governing bodies.

The minister regarded the morphing of the vice-chancellor's role into a chief executive officer – a single point of responsibility – as crucial to ensuring university accountability.[36] The White Paper made clear that councils 'were to delegate clear responsibility and authority to their Chief Executive Officers to implement agreements reached with the Commonwealth, and to hold them responsible for that implementation'. It then recommended that universities undertake internal reviews of their management structures, with a view to the development of 'strong managerial modes of operation, which remove barriers to delegation of policy implementation from governing bodies to Chief Executive Officers and then to other levels'.[37] Marginson and Considine suggest that Dawkins was himself a model of what he wanted vice-chancellors to become:

> Dawkins was to higher education what Treasurer Paul Keating was to financial deregulation, and the then Prime Minister Margaret Thatcher was to British politics: the model neo-liberal executive, forcing through a single-minded reform crusade with a mix of system planning, market rhetoric and the determination to crush all political opposition ... What the senior managers of the universities could not avoid they plainly chose to imitate.[38]

Dawkins believed that he was creating a system that provided universities with freedom to innovate and differentiate within the parameters of the Unified National System and their individual compacts with the Commonwealth.[39] He also wanted to introduce greater competition into the sector, which he achieved through a change to how research funding was allocated. A proportion of higher education funding was withheld to create a pool of research financing, which universities and academics were invited to compete for. The logic of competition has become embedded in the university sector, turning the scarcity of resources into a virtue, as greater competition is assumed to yield greater quality. The other neoliberal logic that was applied to the university sector was the relentless drive for efficiencies – the need to produce more with the same or preferably less investment. The price of public funding in a neoliberal age is the need to continually do more with less. In the case of higher education this meant teaching more students with the same number of, or even better fewer, academics. It meant no new universities were contemplated, even as the number of students continued to climb. Classes increased in size, academic workloads ballooned and university teaching lost its intimacy.

As universities accepted and adjusted to the Unified National System, their internal operations began to mirror the approach to higher education regulation adopted by the government. As government had imposed on universities a system of regulation by strategic plans, targets, budget control and accountability, incentives and competition, universities adopted similar systems for internal governance. Just as government withheld a proportion of higher education funding to incentivise research excellence through competition, so too university chancelleries began to top-slice revenues to create strategic funds, for which different interests would compete to enable their own projects. It was an 'outside-in' form of regulatory influence, which simultaneously strengthened executive power within the university and enabled external regulatory preferences to be transmitted quickly and efficiently throughout the entire institution.[40] Both government and university realised that 'underfunding plus discretionary payments added up to intimate influence'.[41]

Vice-chancellors found themselves in completely new territory, with different relationships to their governing councils, to government and to their own organisations. One commented to Dawkins that the governance changes and the development of a university 'profile' as part of the funding agreement with the government had given him for the first time a clear idea of all of the activity occurring across the university.[42] The need for performance measurement and reporting, along with new regimes of quality assurance and accreditation that were added over the next decade, as well as the imperative to prevail in the competition for scarce funding and international students, saw the size of university chancelleries increase. They acquired chief operating officers, non-academic staff with management skills, and a range of deputy vice-chancellors, vice presidents and pro vice-chancellors with specialised responsibilities for different aspects of university operations. Their task was to implement, monitor and ensure compliance with the growing complex of requirements imposed on the university by the regulatory state. Corporatisation was a fractal process, as lower levels of the university replicated governance systems of the centre. Deans acquired executive authority, strategic funds, budget responsibility and strategic plans, along with their own associate deans and professional staff. Sometimes these were also replicated below them, at school or departmental level. Meanwhile, individual academics found themselves in a new world of compliance and quality assurance. A review of reporting requirements on Australia's universities in 2012 found that they faced forty-six separate data-collecting requirements, and eighteen annual reporting requirements to the Commonwealth Department of Education. It estimated this required 2,000 staff days and $800,000 to $900,000 to comply with for each institution, or 660,000 staff days and $26 million in compliance costs across the sector.[43] In the decade since that review, the compliance requirements and costs have undoubtedly grown substantially. As Hannah Forsyth observes, the monitoring of the quality of outputs has become increasingly dominant: 'Instead of measuring the value of research by what was spent on it, governments decided to measure the quality of what the universities did.'[44]

The Corporate University

The governance changes towards corporatisation in Australia's universities may have happened over time without John Dawkins' zeal. As Sheila Slaughter and Larry Leslie documented in their careful 1997 study *Academic Capitalism*, universities in Britain, the United States and Canada have all shifted towards funding scarcity, competition and more corporate modes of management.[45] What was unique in the Australian experience was the determination and energy of one government minister to bend the country's universities to the neoliberal logic of the new public management – and how quickly he achieved it. The speed is testament to Dawkins' energy and determination as minister, but it also reveals something about the universities. As one close study put it, 'university leaders used the Dawkins reforms as legitimation for an internal revolution which often copied Canberra's much reviled instruments of government: the efficiency saving, the strategic fund, the relative funding model, and the central performance formula.'[46] Some structures of academic collegiality and consensus decision-making, such as academic boards, survived, but were shunted towards the work of upholding academic standards and curricular integrity. Government requirements of accountability and accreditation, however, mean that their original function of self-regulation and quality assurance are no longer trusted.[47] Where academic boards are consulted on matters of university strategy, the strategy has already been designed and agreed by executive processes. The creation of powerful central executives, headed by the vice-chancellor as CEO, supplanted all other older forms of academic governance. Governing councils shrank in size and shifted in composition and role, much more closely resembling corporate boards. Vice-chancellors were no longer elected; they were appointed by councils who were looking for a chief executive officer. Their salaries began to be computed as corporate boards would compute CEO salaries. Other senior executives, such as deans, were appointed, not elected. All were expected to be well versed in institutional management. Academic leadership became a career path.

Without these changes, universities could not have negotiated the shifts in their operating environment that have occurred over the past three decades. As government funding per student has stalled, universities have had to manage a transition towards teaching at scale. With growing demand for international education, Australia's universities have responded with entrepreneurialism and energy. As the competition for research funding intensifies, universities have become more enterprising in seeking commercial partners and philanthropic funding. But here lies a paradox. Where Dawkins believed the shift towards a regulatory relationship between government and universities would allow greater latitude and differentiation, his reforms have had the opposite effect: 'The more governments encourage the deregulation and privatisation of higher education, the less autonomous do the institutions of higher education become.'[48] Dawkins used the lever of funding to bend Australia's universities to his will. But even as government funding becomes a smaller proportion of university budgets, government demands for accountability increase. An escalating spiral between regulation and corporatisation shows few signs of abating.

The growing burden of regulation and accountability requirements suggests that despite universities reporting on more and more of their activities and outcomes, government and society in Australia remain unconvinced of the value of universities. The questions recur in newspapers and conversations: what value do our universities add to the country? Is the payoff to the individual student worth the investment of going to university? Hitherto, universities' efforts to convince the public of their value seem to have had little impact. Their corporatisation has encouraged the perception that their central focus is their own thriving and prestige.

While the Dawkins reforms decisively reshaped the nature and place of universities in Australian life, they were not accompanied by a national conversation about what we want our universities to do, and why. Without a broadly held sense of the value of universities to Australian society, the regulation–corporatisation spiral will continue to spin – to no-one's satisfaction or benefit.

3

Loyalty

IN AUGUST AND November each year, clumps of graduating students and their parents drift through the gothic quadrangles of Australia's oldest universities. The students wear academic gowns over expensive dresses and suits, and mortarboards over professionally coifed hair. They pose in front of dramatic backdrops of carved doorways and arches of discoloured granite and sandstone to be photographed, some by professional photographers, others by parents. The parents are also dressed to the nines, some in suits, others in saris and batik. They have come to realise their investment – a degree for their child from a world-class university that has cost them hundreds of thousands of dollars.

These people embody Australia's most successful new export industry – higher education. Every year, Australia's forty-two universities graduate tens of thousands of students who arrived from and will return to other countries. In 2019, Australia's universities collectively earned $9.9 billion from international students, their revenues from this source having increased by over 10 per cent each year for the previous decade. International student revenue has increased on average five times faster than government support for universities, rising from contributing 17.5 per cent of university finances in 2010 to 27.3 per cent in 2019.[1] This revenue flow has become a major part of the privatisation of the funding of Australia's public university system, helping to lift Australia to fourth spot among the thirty-eight OECD countries for the proportion of private investment in its public higher education sector.

Beyond international students, the forces of academic globalisation are transforming our universities in less obvious but equally profound ways. Academics and academic work have internationalised extensively over the past three decades. The pressure to publish and collaborate internationally, and the lure of international conferences and research, have steadily dragged academics' gaze beyond Australia's borders. Regular publications of global rankings of universities claim to inform Australians of where their universities sit against others around the world. Australian students are themselves attracted to the cloisters of foreign universities: rising numbers are travelling overseas to study as part of their Australian university degree or to complete graduate degrees abroad.

Australia's universities are eager to trumpet the international markers of their success: international fees generated; positions in global rankings; academic prizes gained; research networks joined. But not everyone is comfortable with the internationalisation of Australia's universities. Concerns about the number of foreign students on Australian campuses and in its major cities are regularly rehearsed on the airwaves and in the pages of national newspapers.

When the University of New South Wales conducted a survey on public attitudes towards international students in February 2019, it found 54 per cent of respondents advocated for a limit on the number of foreign students allowed in. The number rose to 62 per cent among eighteen- to thirty-four-year-olds.[2] There is also discomfort with universities' commercial success with international education. In May 2019, the ABC's long-running investigative journalism series *Four Corners* screened a program accusing universities of profiteering from international education. As Australia's borders closed with the onset of the COVID pandemic, this discomfort turned to anger that Australia's universities had allowed themselves to be so exposed to international student revenue. And as Australia's bilateral relationship with China turned sour at the same time, concerns grew about the extensive collaboration between Australian and Chinese academics. Lying just beneath these concerns and criticisms is the question, just whose universities are they anyway?

Academic Globalisation

Universities have always been international institutions, attracting students and academics across borders to join communities of learning. The University of Paris emerged during the twelfth century with a student body organised into four *nationes* reflecting different language groupings: France, Normandy, Picardy and England. The gaining of the status of a university during the Middle Ages meant that the degrees it issued would be recognised internationally by all other universities. Scholars read the works of their counterparts in other countries in Latin, the academic lingua franca. By the fifteenth century, the university as an institutional form had been exported across Europe. From the seventeenth century, the European form of the university was shipped outside of Europe to the Americas. By the nineteenth century it had reached Australia.

Australia's universities were founded on British blueprints and initially staffed with British academics. Their curricula were closely modelled along British lines, as were their philosophies of education, at times creating tension with the strongly vocational ethos of Australia's early universities.[3] However, geographic isolation made regular interactions with an international academic community very difficult. Well into the twentieth century, Australian universities and academics found it difficult and costly to interact with counterparts on the same continent, let alone with those overseas.[4] However, despite these barriers, the internationalist instinct burned strong. Australian academics remained closely attuned to developments in universities overseas and were quick to adopt innovations in research and teaching that they could observe from abroad. Over time, technology began to remove the barriers to international interaction, allowing the internationalist instinct within Australia's universities to express itself fully. Academic globalisation – the increasing impact of international opportunities, developments and standards on all aspects of academic work – has been an accelerating dynamic, particularly over the past thirty years.

Students from Asia began studying at Australia's universities in the 1920s; historian Julia Horne records that N.Y. Shah from Wuhan in China enrolled in the University of Sydney to study teaching in 1923.[5] Numbers began to increase after World War II as decolonisation took hold in Southeast Asia. Aware of the negative perceptions of the White Australia Policy among the elites in Asia's newly independent countries, the Chifley government developed scholarships to support students from Asia studying at Australian universities. It was a policy incorporated into the Colombo Plan by the Menzies government, but both approaches had limited impact on countering negative impressions of Australia's racist immigration policy. Contrary to popular memory, however, Australian government-sponsored international students were greatly outnumbered by privately financed international students studying at Australian universities in the 1950s and 1960s: 'sponsored students under the Colombo Plan and other smaller schemes represented just 23 per cent of the total number of overseas students in tertiary institutions in 1955; this number had dropped to 16 per cent in 1964.'[6] Benefiting from the government's desire to counter negative sentiments over the White Australia Policy, relatively lax visa requirements, and having to pay just 10 per cent of the costs of their courses (the same as Australian students), the number of students from Southeast and South Asia accessing an Australian university education started to grow strongly. There were 925 private overseas students at Australian universities in 1955, whereas there were 3,240 in 1965.[7] Historians of the Colombo Plan have argued that the presence of international students in Australian society played a significant role in changing Australian public attitudes to race, leading to the weakening of the White Australia Policy after 1966 and its dismantling in 1973.[8]

International education moved from a reputation-enhancing sideline to an opportunity to create a new services export sector during the 1980s. Education was identified as an untapped asset that could play a leading role in helping Australia transition from a resources exporter to a services exporter. When the Australian government produced a National Strategy for International Education in 2016, this thinking was prominent: 'Recognised as one of the five super-growth sectors contributing to Australia's transition from a resources-based to a modern services economy, international education offers an unprecedented opportunity for Australia to capitalise on increasing global demand for education services.'[9] The policy changes instituted under the Dawkins reforms provided universities with strong incentives to recruit international students. There would be no upper limit on the numbers universities could recruit; they could retain all income other than a small capital charge; and fees could be set without regulation, considerably above the marginal cost of course delivery. In 1987 universities were earning a 24 per cent margin for international engineering students, 40 per cent on international science students and 56 per cent for international business students.[10] Here was a sector that allowed universities free rein for their entrepreneurial flair and allowed them to keep the rewards of their entrepreneurialism. Numbers of international students on Australian campuses began growing, with the university sector accounting for over two-thirds of all international students coming to Australia. Initially, the largest numbers came from former British Commonwealth countries with long histories of study in Australia: Singapore, Malaysia and Hong Kong. But by the turn of the century, the number of students from China had started to outpace these traditional sources of students. Between 2005 and 2011, the number of Chinese students entering Australian universities jumped 127 per cent, averaging a 13 per cent increase year on year; between 2012 and 2020 they increased another 70 per cent or by an average increase of 11 per cent year on year. The number of Indian students began to increase off a lower base at around the same time, though it dipped after a series of well-publicised attacks on Indian students in Melbourne in 2009. They began to recover soon after, though, rising 412 per cent between 2013 and 2019, or at an average increase of 32 per cent year on year. By 2019, the top seven sources for international students at Australian universities were China (170,786), India (87,085), Nepal (32,152), Malaysia (28,398), Singapore (27,455), Hong Kong (12,813) and Indonesia (12,647).

From a standing start, Australia had captured over 18 per cent of the entire global population of international students by 2019, the third-highest proportion after the United States and the United Kingdom. This performance owed much to several advantages: Australia's universities teach in English; they are located in the region with the highest demand growth for higher education; they are ranked well in global rankings and prestige; Australia is generally seen as safe and welcoming; quality control of higher education is regarded as rigorous; and university fees are considered reasonable by comparison with the top American and British institutions. The entrepreneurial opening of Australian higher education to international students also coincided with a period of rapid growth in Asian economies, and the swift expansion of Asia's middle classes. The deep respect for education among many Asian cultures, coupled with the limited domestic supply of high-quality university education, meant that middle-class parents were prepared to pay significant amounts to educate their children in Australia. Many spent all or most of their life savings, or were prepared to go into debt. Visa settings that permitted international students to work while studying and offered pathways to permanent residency after finishing added to Australia's attractiveness.

The aggregate statistics on international students in Australia hide significant variations within the university sector. International students tend to prefer the higher-ranked institutions, resulting in the five highest-ranked universities (Melbourne, Queensland, Sydney, New South Wales and Monash) capturing nearly one-third of all international students and 44 per cent of all international student revenue.[11] These preference flows are reflected in the wide variation of fees charged for similar degrees. While a business degree will cost $47,700 for an international student attending Southern Cross University, a similar degree will cost $114,100 for an international student choosing to study business at the University of Sydney. Because a university education is a prestige good, higher prices tend to stimulate demand, leading to steadily increasing prices at Australia's highest-ranked universities, and the fastest rates of growth in international students at those universities. The 'big five' highest-ranked universities each earn revenue approaching (or above in the case of Sydney) $1 billion per year from international fees, many times the international fees earned by other Australian universities. Much of this revenue is used to fund research, infrastructure and facilities, leading to steady progress up the global rankings tables. Modelling by Andrew Norton estimates that of the $12.1 billion spent annually on university research in Australia, 27 per cent or $3.3 billion is supplied from international student revenues.[12] A reinforcing cycle has developed: high rankings draw international students; higher margin from their fees is invested in research productivity; leading to higher rankings; stimulating even more demand from international students.[13]

The insistent forces of academic globalisation have been even more compelling for university research than for university education. The internationalisation of research has been a truly global trend, leaving few countries unaffected, but Australia has embarked on research internationalisation with particular enthusiasm. The global average number of international academic publications sits at 35 per cent, yet the proportion of all Australian academic publications with at least one international author is 45 per cent.[14] International law academic Anthea Roberts has mapped global flows of students and ideas to identify a clear international academic hierarchy in which students flow from the periphery (Asia, Africa, Latin America) to the core (Europe and North America), and ideas flow from the core to the periphery.[15] In Roberts' hierarchy, Australia seems to sit between the two, in the semi-periphery: its own students still heading towards the core but able to attract large numbers of students from the periphery. In the world of ideas, Australia's semi-peripheral location seems to have stimulated partnerships and flows in both directions: the top five countries with which Australian researchers partner include countries in both the core and the periphery. Australia also appears to benefit from being part of two of the three major global research clusters: Transpacific, Commonwealth and European.[16]

The internationalisation of Australian research is part of a global trend that has seen the rapid increase of international research collaboration in recent decades, particularly in the science, technical, engineering and medical (STEM) disciplines.[17] Studies show that international research collaboration results in papers that are of higher quality and which are more heavily cited than single-country research. International science specialist Caroline Wagner estimates that internationally co-authored papers are cited at twice the rate on average as single-country authored papers.[18] International collaboration has also been shown to increase academics' research productivity.[19] Individual motivations for academic success will therefore lead scholars to pursue international research collaboration, despite the higher costs and coordination and cultural challenges.[20] Other factors are at work also. As the knowledge frontier recedes, unresolved problems are likely to be too big and complex for a single country's scientists to tackle, while technology eases the barriers of distance: 'International collaboration has increased due to the growing complexity of many research problems, specialisation across different disciplines, the rising cost of research apparatus, and as the ease of modern communication [increases] due to [the] development of new technologies.'[21]

The most rapid growth in Australian researchers' international partnerships came with collaborators in China. In the year prior to the pandemic, the number of Australian scientific publications with a Chinese co-author grew by 13.1 per cent. That year Australia–China co-authorships reached 16.2 per cent of all Australian scientific publications, surpassing Australia–US joint publications (15.5 per cent) to place China as Australia's most significant scientific research collaborator.[22] This appears to have been partly due to the influx of Chinese students onto Australian campuses and partly due to deliberate government strategies. China sits within a small group of developing science and technology powers seeking to leverage international linkages to build domestic STEM capacity. While international collaboration has increased tenfold for scientists from developed countries, it has increased at twice that rate for scientists in the BRICs countries (Brazil, Russia, India and China).[23] Analysis shows that the benefits of international collaboration fall disproportionately to the weaker scientific partner.[24] Many Australian scientists report that where once the benefits of collaboration flowed towards their Chinese collaborators, now Australian researchers are increasingly the net beneficiaries of collaborations with Chinese counterparts. China has funnelled increasing funding into its research-intensive universities, encouraging Chinese scientists to develop international collaborations with scientists in countries with strong scientific cultures as a way of building the strength, capabilities and visibility of its own scientific operations.[25] Australia is currently China's third most regular international research collaborator, rising from fourth in China's collaborator list in 2016.[26] But the encouragement has come from Australia also. From the signing of an Australia–China science and technology cooperation treaty in 1980 to the establishment of an Australia–China Science and Research Fund, Australian governments of both sides have viewed academic collaboration with Chinese counterparts as an important strand in building the bilateral relationship. Showcasing academic and scientific partnerships between Australia and China became a predictable feature of bilateral set pieces when Australian leaders were in China or when Chinese leaders were in Australia.

Assets and Liabilities

The academic globalisation of Australia's universities after 1990 was a process that seemed to have developed by stealth. While the growing ethnic diversity of university campuses was an observable reality for students, the rise of international education as a major export sector was a development few noticed. And beyond the odd speech reference or expo presentation, many Australians would have been unaware of the increasing number, frequency and impact of Australian academics' international research partnerships. While concerns about international students' English proficiency and effects on academic standards had been circulating in Australian society since the 1950s,[27] it took a perfect storm of the closure of Australia's borders as a response to COVID and the rapid unravelling of Australia's bilateral relationship with China to draw sustained and critical attention to the internationalisation of Australia's university sector. The high numbers of Chinese students came to be seen increasingly as an avoidable vulnerability, in which self-interested universities had allowed themselves to become narrowly dependent on a particular source of income, exposing them and the country to financial coercion by China.[28] As China slapped trade restrictions on a range of Australian exports, including barley, coal and lobsters, many commentators expected higher education would be next. Even without formal sanctions, the projected downturn in international student numbers, it was argued, would see Australia's universities more exposed than their counterparts in Europe and North America.[29] Confrontations over political stand-offs in relation to Taiwan and

Hong Kong, which created protests on several campuses, raised concerns about China's political influence over Australia's universities. And increasingly, universities became the focus of rising concerns about China's foreign influence, espionage and intellectual property theft operations in Australia. By engaging in academic globalisation, according to the critics, universities had left Australia open to a range of forms of coercion and exploitation by China.

One anxiety with a long pedigree is that international students diminish the opportunities and access of Australian students to Australia's universities. As the number of Australians qualified for and wanting to attend university began to rise in the 1960s, the persistent concern about 'unmet demand' for university education soon morphed into a conviction that international students were occupying places that could have been filled by Australian students. Responding to these concerns, Minister for Education and Science John Gorton took a submission to Cabinet in 1966 proposing to freeze the number of international students allowed to attend Australian universities.[30] The proposal was rejected by Cabinet, but suspicion that international students were taking places from Australians did not dissipate, emerging most pointedly when anxiety about access to university was most prevalent in society. When John Dawkins proposed allowing universities to recruit international students and keep almost all of the fee income in the 1980s, he was adamant that this could only proceed in tandem with expanding access to university for Australians, precisely because he was worried about the risk that international students might be seen to be occupying places that could have accommodated Australian students.[31] Despite the broad expansion of access to university for Australians that followed the Dawkins reforms, the suspicion that international students are depriving locals of places lingers and emerged powerfully during the pandemic. As closed borders raised the issue of the impact of skills shortages on Australia's economic recovery, some commentators argued that international students were preventing universities from training Australians in needed skills: 'Instead of trying to attract overseas students who take their skills elsewhere, universities could reimagine themselves to invest in local education.'[32]

A variation on this theme – also dating from the 1950s – is that international students erode the academic standards of Australia's universities and compromise the university experience of local students. Complaints that international students lacked requisite English language and academic skills led Commonwealth education authorities to begin developing a standardised English test for overseas students in the 1950s and start to administer the test from the mid-1960s.[33] Despite clear standards required for English proficiency ever since, these complaints have never been allayed. Letters to the newspapers periodically tell stories of Australian students as a minority in classes full of international students who either speak to each other in a language other than English or who lack the English proficiency to participate in class work or group assignments.[34] Another claim, repeatedly made by former federal education minister Alan Tudge, is that universities' giving greater attention to international students has detracted from their primary purpose – the education of Australian students.[35] Consequently, as the borders closed during the pandemic and fears of China sanctioning education rose, there was palpable satisfaction among some that without international students Australia's universities would be forced to turn their attention back to local students: 'if it means our universities can stop being mere finishing schools for the Chinese bourgeoisie and more places are available for Australian students, even working-class ones, then let the Chinese carry out their threats.'[36] When universities began to propose 'secure corridors' to fly international students into Australia and quarantine them, correspondents to newspapers angrily asked why the universities were not directing such resources and creativity towards improving the experience of Australian students.[37]

Negative perceptions of the impact of international students extend beyond campus also. In tones echoing opposition to immigration, critics argue that international education draws more people into Australia's largest cities, increasing the strain on already inadequate infrastructure, driving up property prices and increasing inflation.[38] Others argue that international education exposes students to labour exploitation, creating a low-skilled underclass in Australian society.[39] This, for some, cannot be separated from local unemployment:

Young Australians can't get entry level jobs yet there were 956,773 foreign students in Australia in 2019, most with the right to work. Foreign students and 457 visa holders can be exploited by employers, paid below-award wages and forced to work unacceptable hours, and so are preferred by employers, yet the unions do nothing to stop it.[40]

Opponents of international education are convinced that universities are willing participants in a migration scam, allowing government and business to evade scrutiny over the implications of the high levels of immigration that they favour.[41] The students themselves, allegedly attending university for other motives, are accused of being willing participants in the scam at all points in the 'student life cycle': in the applications process through falsification of academic achievements and English language proficiency; during their studies through contract cheating and plagiarism; and after graduating, when they supposedly fall short of employer expectations.[42] In allegedly turning a blind eye to the migration scam, universities are accused of willingly diluting their own academic standards and integrity to accommodate lucrative international students by tolerating misconduct.[43]

These negative sentiments about international students found a prime ministerial voice just after Australia's borders closed, when Scott Morrison told the media on 3 April 2020, 'if [international students] are not in a position to support themselves, then there is the alternative for them to return to their home countries.'[44] For many international students, the statement confirmed what they suspected was a transactional interest in them by Australia. The national discussion about international students reinforced on both sides the sense that they were commodities, to be denounced or defended based on their impacts on Australian society. Programs such as the ABC's *Four Corners*' 'Degrees of Deception', screened on 20 April 2015, set the tone of a popular meme about international education as a giant scam between universities willing to create loopholes to accommodate poorly qualified but lucrative international students, who then use deception and academic misconduct to navigate their degrees, all to the detriment of Australian students and academic standards. Defenders of international education counter by stressing the positive effects of international students on local economies and the income they generate for the country.[45] Both arguments commodify and homogenise international students, depriving them of their personalities and ambitions and the sacrifices they and their families make.[46] A strong whiff of xenophobia accompanies debate over international education in Australia, including arguments that the students' presence in classrooms opens universities to foreign influence and manipulation; anecdotes that impugn international students' motives, abilities and academic ethics; and charges that they erode academic standards and the experience of Australian students. There is far too little attention given to international students' struggles with isolation, racism and mental health, and to their vulnerability to exploitation and wage theft. These public attitudes to international education manifested in very different governmental responses towards international students during the pandemic. The federal government, more attuned to negative public sentiments about international education, provided no support for international students stranded by closed borders and unable to work to support themselves until June 2021; whereas various state and local governments and universities stepped in to provide significant support to international students in distress and emphasise their importance to Australia.[47]

Australia's universities have not done enough to properly accommodate and absorb the rising numbers of international students on their campuses. Twenty-five years ago, Simon Marginson argued,

> While the growth in international students suggested universities were being 'internationalised', there was little evidence that courses had changed. Globalised education brought different cultural groups into contact on an unprecedented scale, but on the grounds of an Anglo-American-Australian curriculum that Australian universities continued to essentialise as the only possible education.[48]

In the years since, little attention or effort has been directed towards helping international students adapt to Australian university life or encouraging Australian students to get to know them, resulting in enduring cultural divides on university campuses and widespread feelings of marginalisation for international students in and outside of the classroom.[49] Nor has there been any sustained effort to reflect the diversity in the classroom in the teaching curriculum, or to use this cultural diversity as a teaching resource to develop student capabilities to operate cross-culturally. International students are simply expected to understand Australian standards of academic skills and integrity, despite considerable evidence that different cultural approaches to education produce different academic skills and understandings of practices such as copying others' work.[50] Here is a significant challenge that Australia's universities need to take on: convincing the broader public of the non-monetary value of international education for Australia more generally. International student revenues fill the gap between what Australians expect of the quality of their higher education system and what they are prepared to pay for it. Increasing the cultural diversity of the classroom should enhance the educational experience for all. But in order for this to be apparent, universities, too, must work to reshape their curricula to better reflect and realise the international richness of their classrooms and campuses.

Globalism and Nationalism

In October 2018, hawkish defence think tank the Australian Strategic Policy Institute (ASPI) published a paper documenting the Chinese People's Liberation Army's programs for establishing collaboration with Australian universities as a way of accessing cutting-edge dual-use technology.[51] The report gained widespread attention, drawing particular focus to a Chinese government program named 'Thousand Talents', designed to attract top researchers to Chinese universities. In the context of rising concern about China's influence operations in Australia, and sensational allegations of academics in the United States secretly working for Chinese institutions, suspicion quickly settled on Australian universities' extensive research ties to China and thousands of Chinese students. Sensationalist exposés followed, claiming that 'scientists in our universities [are] plugged into a secretive, strategic operation of the Chinese Communist Party'.[52] While some readers saw nothing more than the usual cross-border flows of knowledge, others saw high treason: 'Someone who accepts money from a foreign adversary in exchange for covertly providing that power with technological secrets and intelligence – I believe there is a word for such people.'[53] When some academics and university research institutes urged the government to repair ties with China, they were quickly accused of having succumbed to China's influence operations.[54] Universities' dependence on revenue from Chinese students, it seemed, made them susceptible to selling out Australia's national interests in pursuit of the Chinese student dollar. As the hysteria mounted, there were fears universities would hijack Australia's China policy. 'Unless our federal government better explains the national security risks,' thundered the head of the ASPI, 'Australia's relations with China will be driven by groups interested in economic engagement, not national security.'[55]

There was significant bemusement within Australia's universities. Many academics were surprised to learn that universities had such incipient control of the nation's foreign policy. When federal education minister Dan Tehan announced the creation of a task force to oversee measures to counter foreign interference in Australia's universities, there was a great deal of bewilderment at how quickly the government's policy on research and educational links with China had done an about face. Decades of official encouragement, resourcing and celebration of Australia–China academic linkages had been replaced overnight by suspicion and hostility. Often the alarmist claims about Chinese researchers wanting to steal Australian research were laughable, obviously being made and believed by people with no understanding of the open, collaborative nature of academic research. A large cyber attack on ANU in June 2018 seemed only to amplify the image of universities as Australia's soft underbelly for Chinese influence. Following trends in the United States, attention focused on the dozen Australian universities hosting Confucius Institutes. These were transparently an exercise in 'soft power' by Beijing, willingly accepted by Australian governments during an era in which both China and Australia supported the development of a network of thirty-nine Australian Studies Centres at universities across China – as an exercise in Australian soft power. But in the paranoid spiral that developed after 2018, the Confucius Institutes suddenly morphed in public discussion from showcasing Chinese language and culture into portals for malign Chinese Communist Party influence to infect the nation's soul. The alarm over Confucius Institutes continued to rise, with some arguing that they represented for Beijing 'a breach in the battlefront with Western values'.[56]

Caricatures of universities as fifth-columns for China's influence merged with broader narratives on the disloyalty of Australia's academics. As controversy raged around the ANU's withdrawal from negotiations to establish a program for the teaching of Western civilisation, critics questioned universities' reluctance to teach Australia's own culture while they seemed more than happy to promote the understanding of China's culture through Confucius Institutes.[57] For Liberal senator Jim Molan, universities had become hotbeds of 'narrow, anti-Australian views'.[58] While Australian academics appeared more than willing to criticise aspects of their own country's history and culture, universities fell under suspicion for self-censoring when it came to China. Molan's colleague Senator James Paterson told Sky News, 'our universities have an extraordinary amount of their revenue from international students, particularly from China ... It's not a bad thing inherently, but it does make our universities highly sensitive to criticism of China and the impact that could have on student flows.'[59] In July 2019, a stand-off occurred on the University of Queensland campus when a group of protesters against China's imposition of a national security law in Hong Kong was confronted by counter-protesters advocating for the imposition of the law. When one of the pro–Hong Kong protesters – student and university senate office holder Drew Pavlou – was suspended for two years for misconduct in May 2020, the case came to national attention, with many critics seizing it as an example of a university's willingness to restrict freedom of speech in order to protect its revenue from Chinese students.[60] Two months later, the University of New South Wales removed an article critical of China's human rights record from one of its websites, only compounding critics' claims that international student fees were a higher priority to universities than freedom of speech. Unspecified claims that Chinese students were bullying academics into aligning classroom discussions with China's official stance on territorial issues added to perceptions among some that Beijing's influence over Australian universities was pervasive and growing.[61]

Whose Universities?

Suddenly, the work of Australia's universities was no longer 'academic' and irrelevant; China's interest in building partnerships, access and influence on campuses showed that what was happening there was deeply significant and valuable to national life. Universities were obviously the crucibles of 'our' knowledge and technology, paid for by the taxpayer and therefore subject to Australia's proprietorial rights. When acting education minister Stuart Robert cancelled six peer-reviewed Australian Research Council grants in December 2021 on 'national interest' grounds, the decision was explained as ensuring that 'taxpayer-funded Australian government research funding is directed to areas of national importance and delivers public value'.[62] Whether or not Australia's stocks of knowledge held in its universities were accumulated through international partnerships and information flows, longstanding academic practices of open publishing and peer review of research, and the regular cross-fertilisation of ideas at international conferences and symposia, now there was an imperative to ensure Australia's knowledge was not stolen or used contrary to the national interest. The abrupt securitisation and nationalisation of their work left most Australian academics astonished. Academic work by nature spans geographic and temporal boundaries. It cannot exist apart from hundreds of global disciplinary communities, which assess, review, draw on, refute and critique the work of thousands of academics within their own disciplines. To suddenly draw proprietorial and national security boundaries around this practice strikes most academics as profoundly ignorant of the very nature of the academic enterprise. But from beyond the campus, drawing national interest criteria around university research was an imperative. The only controversy seemed to be over whether Australia's universities were naive dupes at the mercy of the Chinese Communist Party, or willing conduits, allowing the siphoning away of Australia's knowledge in return for the bounty flowing in from Chinese students.

Starting in mid-2018, the Australian government began to enact a series of laws, regulations, guidelines and inquiries aimed at protecting Australia from foreign interference and intellectual property theft. Although universities were not the only subjects of these measures, it is remarkable how consistently they focused on universities. While the *National Security Legislation Amendment (Espionage and Foreign Interference) Act 2018* and the Critical Infrastructure Bill 2018 applied to a range of institutions, the 2019 University Foreign Interference Taskforce and 2021 joint parliamentary inquiry into foreign interference in universities were specifically targeted at universities – no other institution was singled out. The 2020 *Australia's Foreign Relations (States and Territories) Act 2020* was amended at the last minute to include public universities within its remit. Under the *Foreign Relations* scheme, universities are required to report all foreign 'arrangements' with 'non-autonomous' institutions to the government, which publishes them on a website and provides the foreign minister with the ability to cancel any arrangements without recourse or explanation. The result was a bureaucratic nightmare for Marise Payne's department to administer and a huge amount of work and expense for Australia's universities; to date, no university's reported foreign arrangement has been halted or cancelled. The 2021 refresh of the University Foreign Interference Taskforce guidelines required universities to collect information on the foreign engagements of all staff as well as provide training and information on the dangers of foreign interference. The regulations and requirements piled up, uncoordinated, despite no case of covert foreign interference or theft of critical technology coming to light.

While governments in the United States, the United Kingdom and Europe had also begun moving in this direction, Australia stood out for the range, number and intrusiveness of the foreign interference requirements that were being imposed on its universities. A new national security regime was descending on centuries of academic internationalism.

When Australia's borders opened again in December 2021, the era of the nation's freewheeling academic internationalism had come to an end. International students began to return, but many stayed away, continuing their studies online or choosing other study destinations due to concerns about how Australia had responded to international students during the pandemic. Higher education analyst Angel Calderon predicts weaker growth in international education revenues into the future, posing real challenges for universities in containing the growth in their expenditure.[63] Some university leaders warn that the multiple and overlapping foreign interference requirements will have a chilling effect on international academic collaboration. So while 2022 saw yet more rises in the global rankings of Australia's 'big five' universities, the prospect of lower international student revenues and a flattening of international research collaborations could see the virtuous circle between international students, research and rankings begin to unravel. Perhaps then China's actual and perceived interest in Australia's universities may begin to wane. If this happens, will Australia's universities still be seen as repositories of knowledge vital to the country's national interests?

4

Integrity

THE MOST EVOCATIVE image of the university in the public mind is that of the cloister. Reproduced in university planning and architecture across the globe, the cloister is the most obvious legacy of the modern university's origins in the monasteries of medieval Europe. In Europe's ancient universities scattered through medieval towns, college and university buildings face away from the street, instead focusing on quadrangles, squares and lawns. Newer universities occupy one or more campuses, banishing the world from the carefully curated landscapes and buildings intended to nurture and inspire the intellect. The function of the cloister for the university, as for the monastery, is to separate particular devotions and practices from the hubbub of daily life; to enable quiet, contemplative discussion and thought free from the demands of the mundane world. Here lies one reason for the popular use of the term 'academic' as a synonym for irrelevant – a widespread if grudging acceptance that what happens in universities occurs on a different plane from the practical pressures, dilemmas and pleasures that fill the streets, homes and supermarkets beyond the cloisters.

If that is the popular expectation, it is certainly not the reality in modern Australian life. The past twenty years have seen a rising tide of controversy over what happens, should happen and supposedly happens inside the country's university cloisters. Far from being 'academic', meaning irrelevant, a series of controversies over student protests, cancelled events, political alignments and academic sackings have shown that what happens on Australian campuses is of intense interest to the broader society. These controversies show a seldom-acknowledged belief that universities and what they do are vital to the common good and the moral tenor of Australian society; and that these supposedly irrelevant institutions have significant actual and potential influence beyond their campus limits.

Public concern over the politicisation of university affairs in Australia dates back to the 1950s, when disputes arose over the appointments of historian Russel Ward and philosopher Frank Knopfelmacher, and the disciplining of philosopher Sydney Sparkes Orr.[1] In the febrile political environment of the early Cold War, Ward's appointment to the New South Wales Institute of Technology was vetoed by the vice-chancellor, allegedly due to Ward's left-leaning politics; Knopfelmacher's appointment to the University of Sydney was campaigned against by the academic staff union due to his anti-communist convictions, while Orr claimed to be the victim of ideological bias in an attempt to avoid sexual misconduct allegations. Since then, politics has come to be a staple part of university life. But the cadence of the academic controversies and the pitch of the outrage has escalated in the past two decades. When a controversial event on a campus hits the headlines, two tribes take to the field, each having honed now familiar interpretations and culprits and sharpened accusations against the other side. What has now become widely referred to as the 'culture wars' is animated by two incompatible views of the broad social purpose of the university in modern Australia: one which sees the university as the bastion of traditional Western values; and the other which believes the university is a vehicle for progressive social change. Each accuses the other of politicising the university. While one accuses 'academics' as a general category of being too progressive, the other accuses universities of being not progressive enough.[2]

Underlying these different views is a common concern over both what is done and how it is done within Australia's campuses. Ultimately what is at stake in the culture wars is a set of disagreements over the integrity of the academic enterprise as it is currently conducted in Australia's universities. What each side decries about Australia's universities boils down to academic practices, rights and responsibilities, and whether or not these are being properly observed or have been perverted and undermined. These are not disputes and accusations that are unique to this country; indeed, it is quite clear that the inspirations, arguments and language of controversies over the academic integrity of Australia's universities have originated in the United States and the United Kingdom. Where our antipodean controversies have followed the logic and argumentation of American and British counterparts and where they have diverged tells us important things about the contemporary role of universities in Australian life.

The March of the Progressives

A regular allegation in the letters and columns of Australia's conservative press is that the institutions of our society are being taken over by a shadowy green-left progressive movement with its origins in the nation's universities. Across Australia's campuses, we are warned, partisans of diversity and minority rights have colonised our institutions of higher learning, stamping out contrary views in increasingly totalitarian ways. Their targeting of universities is deliberate and Leninist; according to Jennifer Oriel,

> Tyrannical leaders often target the intellectual class because it is in the mind, in the world of ideas, that culture is created. The purpose of the university is to nourish higher learning so the finest minds can cultivate the flourishing of culture and the renewal of civilisation as each generation passes through the cloisters. However, in recent years the revolution on campuses across the West has led to dulled minds and coarsened appetites so political violence is viewed as retributive justice. The silencing of dissent has become a mark of progressive pride and an opportunity for like-minded leftists to bond over a common enemy, the dissident.[3]

The result, apparently, has been to create an intellectual environment in universities akin to the 'authoritarian aridity and puerility of theological study in the Middle Ages'.[4] Others warned that academics had fallen under the sway of a 'divisive ideology which pits us against each other on the basis of our immutable characteristics', which is ultimately corrosive of our national cohesion.[5] Within these terrifying institutions, students are evidently 'brainwashed' and placed in 'ideological straitjackets'; no wonder then that universities are the common source of both 'fake news' and 'identity politics'.[6]

Since so many of the nation's youth go to university, it appears inevitable to some that they are being indoctrinated with leftist ideals. A poll carried out in 2018 by the Centre for Independent Studies reported that '58 per cent of Australian millennials – those born between 1980 and 1996 – have a favourable view of socialism, with only 18 per cent having an unfavourable one.'[7] The left-wing bias of Australia's universities can only be of such concern to some citizens, precisely because they are believed to have such a powerful influence on Australian society. Thus the apparent decline in the standards of Australia's schooling system can be traced directly to the leftist dogma that now dominates the university education of our teachers.[8] The structuring of university curricula around identity politics and minority causes is apparently creating in Australia a censorious, judgemental intellectual elite motivated to discipline the rest of society to respect their own moral causes and is caustically dismissive of the intelligence of anyone who might disagree with them.[9] That universities are teaching doctrines so out of step with the presumed views of mainstream Australia has raised inevitable questions of why they were being supported by taxpayer dollars: 'Australia's universities are facing a serious reputational crisis. The more universities become aligned with a single line of political thought, the more the community will wonder, rightly, why billions of taxpayer dollars fund these institutions.'[10]

So for one tribe, intellectual conformity is descending over Australia's universities. Free thinking has been replaced by a 'competition' to toe the conventional, mandated line, apparently making Australia's university campuses more like those in China.[11] The pursuit of knowledge and truth is increasingly being subdued by the urge for consensus.[12] Academics seem to line up behind progressive causes, opposing climate change sceptic Bjorn Lomborg opening a research centre at the University of Western Australia and supporting strikes in favour of climate action.[13] Once again, conformity on campus fosters conformity off campus, driving and reflecting a broader crisis in civic debate.[14] The presumption that political commitments shape academic opinions has led to a questioning of academic judgements and pronouncements. Commentators ridiculed academics who predicted hundreds of thousands of deaths from COVID-19,[15] amid an alleged broader societal collapse in trust in the views of academics and experts.[16]

These pronouncements on the politicisation and decline of Australia's universities have not gone unanswered. Carolyn Evans, vice-chancellor of Griffith University, has observed that 'there is almost always a moral panic about young people, what goes on at universities, and the general end of civilization.'[17] International studies show that the political alignments of university graduates do not differ significantly from those of the same age cohorts who do not attend university.[18] Queensland University of Technology vice-chancellor Margaret Sheil scoffed at claims of indoctrination of whole generations of young Australians: 'I suspect there would be less concern about universities' capacity to influence the politics of the next generation if it was recognised how little influence we actually have.'[19] Others turned to history and the thrall of the mundane to deflate the alarmism:

> In the early 1970s, the Faculty of Arts and the Department of Government at the University of Sydney were hotbeds of communist agitators. Arts was controlled by Marxists, who were in constant dispute with the running dog imperialist Trotskyists at the School of Government. Meanwhile, at University of NSW, the Maoists were in the ascendancy … Despite the indoctrination, within a few years of graduating, most students had grown up and become happy little capitalists. By middle age, most had stopped listening to and watching the ABC and we now start our day reading this august publication [*The Australian*] front to back.[20]

Other commentators derided claims that all universities, in their vastness and complexity, could be taken over by a single point of view: 'As though the broad-based behemoths most universities have become are defined by pockets of Arts faculty-driven anti-Coalition sentiment that cling to life in some institutions. They might at times be loud, but they do not define the sector as a whole, nor do they limit its importance to the nation.'[21] There was also scepticism about the government's commitment to free speech against leftist orthodoxies but its unwillingness to countenance critical consideration of national symbols, such as Anzac Day.[22] Questions have been asked about whether it was universities or their critics who were more out of touch with mainstream opinion.[23] And it was pointed out that universities' pivotal role in responding to COVID-19 showed that they had not surrendered their commitment to truth, objective knowledge and rationality.[24]

If It Ain't Woke

Nothing so clearly illustrates the American origins of the belief in the progressive takeover of Australia's universities than the gradual mainstreaming of the word 'woke' in Australian public discourse, along with well-worn American puns such as 'the great awokening'.[25] As America's cities were convulsed by protests over the murder of George Floyd in mid-2020, and a movement to tear down statues associated with slavery and colonialism in America and Britain began, commentators drew hysterical parallels between 'the woke agenda' and the Cultural Revolution in China.[26] The term 'woke' derives from the African American community, where it was first used in the 1940s to refer to being aware of what was happening in one's community, particularly in relation to racism and injustice. The term seems to have gained popularity after Erykah Badu's 2008 song 'Master Teacher', which couched the term as meaning 'self-aware – questioning the dominant paradigm and striving for something better'.[27] Soon after, the word appears to have been picked up by conservative commentators and used as a term of derision and condemnation. 'Woke' replaces the term 'political correctness', also an import from the United States.[28] The stand-off between the two sides is a direct evolution of a divide that occurred on American college campuses in the 1960s, when intellectuals such as Leo Strauss and Norman Podhoretz reacted in disgust at what they believed was the moral relativism of progressive movements for social change, minority rights and multiculturalism. Soon to be labelled 'neoconservatives', many of these thinkers were particularly contemptuous towards universities for falling to postmodernism and moral relativism, rather than standing firm for objectivity, rationalism and disinterested inquiry.[29] A pivotal part in renewing attention to the role of universities in promoting postmodernism and moral relativism was played by Strauss's student Allan Bloom, who published the bestselling *The Closing of the American Mind* in 1987. Bloom's charge that American universities had abandoned the Western scholarly and philosophical tradition for progressive social causes electrified conservative America and gradually spread across the anglophone world.[30]

Bloom's critical stance on universities and the more recent alarm over a woke cultural revolution were most eagerly transmitted to Australia by News Corp's print and broadcast mastheads, *The Australian* and Sky News, as well as by the libertarian think tank the Institute for Public Affairs (IPA). The IPA took to conducting 'audits' of free speech and 'political correctness' at Australia's universities on an annual basis from 2016, and using its analysis to spread horror through News Corp outlets about what was being taught to the nation's youth:

> … the audit found that 572 subjects, or 44 per cent of the 1181 subjects analysed, were concerned with identity politics, while a further 380 subjects featured critical race theory – a US-born framework for studying race and power responsible for coining the concepts 'white privilege' and 'structural

racism'. About 25 per cent of subjects were focused specifically on gender issues. In contrast, a mere quarter of English literature subjects involved the study of great works comprising the Western canon, while just 23 per cent of history subjects dealt with the history of Western civilisation ranging from Ancient Greece to the modern world. In the political sciences, 10 per cent of subjects offered taught students about the history of ideas and political thought. Freedom, a key tenet of the study of social sciences, was also in just 10 per cent of the 524 possible subjects.[31]

These reports inevitably provoked barrages of outraged letters to the editor, their authors striving to outdo each other in fulminating against the progressive takeover and intellectual impoverishment of Australia's universities. It did not take long for Janet Albrechtsen to solemnly proclaim a 'free speech crisis on campus'.[32]

The central claim seemed to be that alarming trends in America and Britain, such as hauling down statues, rioting, deplatforming and howling down 'non-woke' academics, were making their way to Australia. Director at the Centre for Independent Studies Tom Switzer warned that 'cancel culture' – a 'phenomenon by which anyone in public life, the media or academe who refuses to subscribe to the extreme leftist orthodoxies of a militant and vocal minority are "cancelled"' – was on its way to Australia.[33] His fears seem to have been stoked by developments such as La Trobe University's decision to withdraw an invitation to speak to controversial sex therapist Bettina Arndt in July 2018 – a decision the university reversed shortly afterwards.[34] By 2018 it was clear that members of the federal government had picked up the logic and language of the 'woke crisis' at Australia's universities. Multicultural affairs minister Alan Tudge accused his alma mater, the University of Melbourne, of promoting socially divisive 'identity politics' around a particular theatre production in June 2018.[35] Energy minister Josh Frydenberg lamented Australian universities' 'long march to the left'.[36] Interventions such as this have prompted political philosopher Greg Melluish to speculate that the News Corp/IPA campaign was potentially changing the nature of conservative politics: 'There is a growing tension between classical liberals who invoke the reasonable principles of free speech, intellectual inquiry and neutral government, and those who advocate a more robust attack against the quasi-religious doctrine of wokeism.'[37]

But amid the hyperbole and sense of impending crisis, it is important to acknowledge that the claims made about the politicisation of Australian campuses are not completely baseless. When the University of Melbourne opened the Robert Menzies Institute in early 2022, protesters aggressively prevented guests from accessing the events until security guards could restore order and police were called. The chants of the protesters echoed many of the themes that universities were being accused of promoting by conservative commentators, such as opposition to racism, sexism and homophobia. It was hard to listen to these protesters and not be struck by the irony of these students at one of the country's most exclusive educational institutions railing against social structures of tradition, privilege and intolerance. Like their conservative critics, these protesters can trace their origins to the hyper-charged campus confrontations of the 1960s. University students were at the vanguard of the 'new social movements' that mushroomed during the decade to contest not only existing patterns of power and privilege but also prevailing methods of attaining, holding and contesting power. Across Australia's campuses, students established forms of egalitarian relationships and decision-making that were intended to be 'prefigurative', building through their actions new forms of just social relations within the shell of the old.[38] It was no accident that universities were the growth beds of the new movements for racial and sexual justice, which gained their potency from 'cognitive mobilisation', 'the ability to understand and comprehend politics and political change in abstract and theoretical ways – due largely to the greater access to education in modern societies'.[39]

Participation in such movements provided motivation and ideas to writers, who became the theorists of the new social movements. In the words of Verity Burgmann,

> Intellectuals do not, in the main, invent liberating ideas and impose them on people who then form social movements; rather, intellectually trained people are important in articulating and embellishing ideas that are being worked out in practice, in and by the movements themselves, a process which then aids the further development of the movement.[40]

One such intellectual was Brazilian educational theorist Paulo Freire, who argued that universities reflected and reinforced society's oppressive structures 'by ensuring students learned established ideas, and by granting them no space in which to question them, society's norms would be continually maintained'.[41] Fortified by thinkers such as Freire, Herbert Marcuse and Jürgen Habermas, academics and students came to see education as a powerful means of promoting positive political and social change. Intellectual movements such as postmodernism empowered an attack on established systems of knowledge and scholarship that were argued to be key to maintaining systems of privilege and oppression. University of California president Clark Kerr warned that 'while most acknowledge that the traditional university was partially politicised already, postmodernism will further raise questions of whether the critical function of the university is based on political orientations rather than non-political scientific analysis'.[42] The major shift was the view that the purpose of academic work was to support and achieve progressive social and political change. This had major implications for conceptions of the nature of academic inquiry. For philosopher John Searle, postmodernism became a means to reject the public, rational creation and critique of knowledge as a prelude to advancing particular social and political agendas through academic teaching and research: 'They sought a refutation of the Western Rationalistic Tradition that would justify a revised conception of education that they already found appealing'.[43]

However, acknowledging that political and social agendas shape curriculum in some parts of Australian university campuses is a long way from predicting that universal thought-policing, radical identity assertion and divisive campaigning has, or is about to, take over whole universities across Australia. The caricatures painted by both sides in the culture wars are unrecognisable to anyone who spends a significant amount of time on campus in modern Australia.

What unites the fringes of both sides in the culture wars, though, is their disgust at the modern Australian university. For conservatives, universities have abandoned intellectual rigour, the search for truth, the welcome of a diversity of viewpoints, and a respect for the intellectual heritage of Western society.[44] For progressives, universities are institutions of corporate greed, privilege, patriarchy, racism and 'kyriarchy' – a social system built around domination and oppression.[45] Although they are diametrically opposed in their views of what universities are for, both sides of the culture wars clearly set very high standards for what is done at Australia's universities and how it is done. Both lament universities' supposed abdication of an intellectual and moral leadership role in Australian society; and both visions of the proper role for universities in society appear to be grounded on a liberal vision of higher education – as educating for the type of society they want Australia to be. Both sides are as dismissive of a vocational rationale for higher education as they are contemptuous of each other. Underneath all of the *Sturm und Drang* of the culture wars over modern campus politics may just lie a clear, common vision of the role of universities in Australian life.

Cry Freedom

So often the claim and counterclaim that animates the campus culture wars revolves around a value that sits at the centre of the viability of the university as an institution. In controversy after controversy, one side accuses the other of threatening, eroding or perverting academic freedom. A diverse range of events all seem to be reduced to assaults on this sacred academic principle. Student newspaper *Honi Soit* publishes and then retracts a story on two University of Sydney academics with links to a Chinese talent recruitment program.[46] A University of Melbourne philosopher is targeted in an open letter from 150 colleagues who charge her with promoting a 'harmful ideology'.[47] An ANU student union blocks the Australian Defence Force from setting up a stall on Open Day.[48] A University of Queensland student is suspended for criticising the university's links to China.[49] James Cook University sacks Professor Peter Ridd, who publicly criticises the findings of colleagues about the effects of climate change on the Great Barrier Reef.[50] The constant pressure on universities to contribute to national economic outcomes stifles free and diverse academic inquiry.[51] 'Silencing behaviours' intimidate academics and students to dissuade them from voicing their views.[52] All of these diverse cases, taking place over a four-year period at Australian universities, have led to dire warnings that academic freedom or freedom of speech are under threat on Australian campuses.

Academic freedom is a principle that is indispensable to the work of any university, 'the bedrock upon which a healthy university rests, and from which a vibrant educational community grows ... without it the university undermines its own integrity, legitimacy and central mission'.[53] The practice of unimpeded free and open inquiry is regarded as the public university's central contribution to a liberal democracy by acting as 'the critic and conscience of society' and a repository of public knowledge and scholarship.[54]

Academic freedom can be traced back to one of the founding acts of creating the modern university: the promulgation in 1155 by Holy Roman Emperor Frederick Barbarossa of the edict known variously as *Authentica Habita* or *Privilegium Scholasticum* setting out the rights and privileges of students and scholars at the University of Bologna. The edict guaranteed for members of the academic community exemption from civil laws and privileges similar to those held by the clergy; freedom of movement for academic purposes; immunity from the right of reprisal; and the right to be tried by members of the academic community rather than by civil authorities.[55] This ancient principle began to be codified in the German academic tradition in the late eighteenth century, which maintained that the search for truth depended on the freedom to teach (*Lehrfreiheit*) and learn (*Lernfreiheit*). Academic freedom specialist Adrienne Stone defines the modern conception of academic freedom as resting on three principles: the freedom of research and teaching; institutional autonomy of the university; and an appropriate level of academic governance of universities.[56] Australia's *Higher Education Support Act 2003*, which licences and regulates the country's universities, requires them to uphold 'free intellectual inquiry in relation to learning, teaching and research' as a condition of being able to operate as a university.[57] The principle is also variously written into individual university statutes, codes of conduct and enterprise bargaining agreements.

As many academics lament, the principle of academic governance of Australia's universities has been eroded by the government-mandated 'corporatisation' of university management structures.[58] In its place, universities have preserved a practice that protects the freedom of academics to criticise university governance, a right that most exercise on a regular basis.[59] While academic boards have been sidelined from the central responsibility in governance they once played, they still perform important roles in ensuring academic standards. There is also some doubt over the extent to which university autonomy exists in reality, given the increasingly detailed regulation of their activities by governments. But the essence of guaranteeing free and open inquiry is critical to the purpose, operation and integrity of the academic enterprise, and should rightly be a source of passionate controversy when it is seen to be threatened. Each time controversy arises over academic freedom, it is critical that it is debated and resolved in ways that preserve and clarify its core principles and rationales. Within universities it is important to consistently distinguish between academics' right to freedom of intellectual inquiry and instruction, and academic self-interest – the often-presumed right to carry out their professional duties any way they wish.[60] It is also crucial to emphasise that the right to academic freedom is contingent on adherence to counterpart responsibilities: 'scholars and scientists are free to explore and express ideas *within* the limits set by the stringent demands of rigour and objectivity to which they are subject.'[61] Indeed, many of the institutions that are part of academic life, from peer review to ethics committees to the replicability of experiments and the publishing of data, are directed towards enforcing the rules of academic life and disputation. Academic responsibilities are often lost in the heat of controversies over academic freedom, but are equally crucial to the work of universities: 'honesty, accuracy, fairness, avoidance of fabrication and the like … all of these are necessary conditions for the growth of knowledge through *disciplined* inquiry.'[62] Strict rules of academic conduct are also necessary for the orderly and collegial operation of the critical, disputatious communities that are our universities.

Trouble on Ramsay Street

At the start of June 2018, the chancellor and vice-chancellor of ANU announced that they were breaking off negotiations with the Ramsay Centre over a donation supporting the teaching of a degree in Western civilisation. After six months of negotiations, the university argued that it was unable to accommodate the Ramsay Centre's requirement that it would have a say in the staffing and curriculum decisions of the proposed degree, because these were inconsistent with the principles of academic freedom.[63] Unease about the negotiations among the ANU community had increased following the publication of an article in the journal *Quadrant* by former prime minister Tony Abbott, a member of the Ramsay Centre Board. The article began by bemoaning that educational grounding in the history and culture of the West was vanishing from modern universities, 'starting with the cradle of civilisation and moving through Greece and Rome to the story of England and the birth of the modern world, its triumphs and travails'.[64] This narrative had been replaced by a curriculum 'pervaded by Asian, indigenous and sustainability perspectives' leading to a situation where 'almost entirely absent from the contemporary educational mindset was any sense that cultures might not all be equal and that truth might not entirely be relative'. As an explanation for this, he cited 'O'Sullivan's law': 'Every organisation that's not explicitly right-wing, over time becomes left-wing.' Abbott summed up the animating vision for what was being negotiated:

> The key to understanding the Ramsay Centre for Western Civilisation is that it's not merely *about* Western Civilisation but *in favour* of it. The fact that it is 'for' the cultural inheritance of countries such as ours, rather than just interested in it, makes it distinctive. The fact that respect for our heritage has largely been absent for at least a generation in our premier teaching and academic institutions makes the Ramsay Centre not just timely but necessary.[65]

He closed the essay announcing the impending successful conclusion of negotiations with the ANU, providing details of the approach to teaching a new Bachelor of Western Civilisation and claiming that 'a management committee including the Ramsay CEO and also its academic director will make staffing and curriculum decisions'.

The ANU's withdrawal from negotiations with the Ramsay Foundation took the furore over Australia's universities to a new height of intensity and animus. 'What kind of society undermines itself like this?' thundered the editorial in the *Australian Financial Review*.[66] A University of Sydney history professor likened *The Australian*'s foreign editor's comment on the ANU decision to Norwegian mass killer Anders Breivik's political views.[67] Railing against the 'self-loathing' of Australia's academics, another commentator sneered that the ANU dean participating in the negotiations 'specialises in "gender and labour, prostitution, war and – society, ethnic and religious issues"'.[68] Australian universities were accused of hypocrisy, for rejecting the study of Western civilisation while welcoming centres studying Chinese or Islamic civilisations.[69] Head of the Menzies Research Centre Nick Cater resurrected the label of 'denaturalised intellectuals' to describe 'the unhappy victims of the cultural cringe, isolated and alienated from their own country. Their thinking is clouded by the unsavoury interpretation of the Australian story that pervades history faculties and seeps out through other branches of the humanities'.[70]

Stung by the intensity of the response to their decision, the ANU's leaders took to the media to explain it. Rather than caving to the objections of their supposedly left-wing staff, they argued,

> We withdrew from negotiations because there were irreconcilable differences over the governance of the proposed program, not its substance. We were willing to accept the Ramsay Centre having a voice in curriculum design and staff appointments. But only a voice, not a controlling influence. From the outset, however, the centre has been locked into an extraordinarily prescriptive micro-management approach to the proposed program, unprecedented in our experience, embodied in a draft memorandum of understanding of about 30 pages, with another 40 pages of detailed annexures. It has insisted on a partnership management committee to oversee every aspect of the curriculum and its implementation, with equal numbers from the Ramsay Centre and ANU, meaning an effective Ramsay veto.[71]

In a telling paragraph, Chancellor Gareth Evans and Vice-Chancellor Brian Schmidt placed the ultimate explanation on fundamentally incompatible views about the nature of the university:

> It became clear that there are fundamental differences in our respective conceptions of the role of a university. The centre has gone so far as to insist on the removal of 'academic freedom' as a shared objective for the program: this remains in the draft MOU as an ANU objective, not a Ramsay one. For us, academic freedom doesn't mean freedom to underperform or to teach without regard to the disciplines or agreed objectives of a particular syllabus. But it does mean appointment or retention of staff on the basis of their demonstrated academic merit, not political or ideological preference.[72]

Their explanation found few listeners among the enraged culture warriors. But the episode does reveal crucial insights into prominent understandings and misunderstandings about what universities do and how they should do it.

The promoters of the Ramsay Centre for Western Civilisation were evidently inspired by a nineteenth-century Oxbridge ideal of a classical education, in which the close study of Ancient Greek and Roman texts in their original languages was believed to foster the cultural and moral discernment necessary in society's leaders. The manifesto for this model of a university education was penned by John Henry Newman in a series of lectures, published as *The Idea of a University*.[73] This impulse was modernised in the United States in the years following World War I, when Columbia

University was the first to introduce a program in 'Western Civilization' in 1919, which would feature the sequential study of a pre-determined course of 'great books' of the Western canon. The concept became broadly popular across the United States, inspired by a retrospective admiration for the Victorian ideal of a classical education, and a prospective assertion of Western liberal culture against the threats of totalitarianism and communism.[74] As the onset of the Cold War confronted liberal America with the twin threats of McCarthyism within and communism without, an intellectual movement developed that valorised the teaching of the great works of Western civilisation as a way of fostering 'open minds' in a liberal society against the closed minds of totalitarianism and red-scaremongering.[75] The popularity of great books courses declined in the 1960s as the undergraduate curriculum became increasingly devoted to majors and minors, electives, specialisation, and the imparting of critical thinking and independent study to students.[76]

It was this curricular displacement that Allan Bloom railed against in *The Closing of the American Mind*. The subtitle of his book, *How Higher Education Has Failed Democracy and Impoverished the Souls of Today's Students*, signalled a clear connection in his mind between what was happening on campus and what he saw as the impoverishment and decline of American civic values and political life. Bloom's followers, including the enthusiasts of the Ramsay Centre, drew the immediate corollary: that only by restoring the appropriate teaching of the Western canon in our universities can we start to arrest the erosion of our civic and political ideals. Herein lies a deep paradox that underpins the Western civilisation agenda. On the one hand, the case for the study of it is based on the view that it has delivered humanity's greatest achievements. Doing his best Monty Python impersonation, Abbott ventured to conjure the thoughts of the departed Paul Ramsay:

> To the question, 'What has Western Civilisation ever done for us?' [Paul Ramsay] would have ventured: not so much, perhaps, save for the rule of law, representative democracy, freedom of speech, of conscience and religion, liberal pluralism, the prosperity born of market capitalism, the capability born of scientific rigour, and the cultivation born of endless intellectual and artistic curiosity.[77]

To this list other Ramsay Centre supporters add the 'outstanding Western scientific, technological and engineering culture that has given the world transformative engines, instant global communications, air travel, antibiotics, anaesthetics, genomics, the capacity to gaze into deep space and many other pragmatic, monetizable achievements'.[78] Paradoxically, however, this triumphalist case for the study of Western civilisation is premised on a deep cultural pessimism: that the same culture which has produced all of these achievements has also produced ideas such as cultural relativism, critical theory, multiculturalism and minority rights, which are leading to the decadence and decline of Western civilisation.[79]

The result of this paradox is that proponents of the study of Western civilisation advocate that its great books have to be uncritically accepted and studied in a particular way: in Abbott's words, 'it's not merely about Western Civilisation but *in favour* of it.' While Abbott concedes, reluctantly and briefly, 'and, yes, [the] capacity to criticise itself' it is clear from the tenor of his article that any critique of the great books needs to be closely circumscribed. This pre-emptively uncritical approach to the study of the Western canon seems to be wary of subjecting it to the critical, sceptical methods that are undermining our social and cultural cohesion. Proponents of the Ramsay Centre were particularly angered when critics pointed out that the Western tradition also included slavery, religious intolerance, colonialism and exploitive industrialisation. The unwillingness to contemplate any critical stance on Western civilisation seems to have been borne out by the Ramsay Centre's approach to negotiations with the ANU:

> It has been unwilling to accept our draft curriculum and has refused to accept our preferred name for the degree, Western civilisation studies. While acknowledging that any curriculum would have to be endorsed by ANU's academic board, it has made clear that to be acceptable to the Ramsay Centre it would have to find favour with the joint management committee, whose representatives wanted to sit in the classes that we teach and undertake 'health checks' on courses and teachers.[80]

With supporters of the Ramsay Centre believing that 'none of the humanities faculties at our major public universities were fit for the task' of teaching the Western canon in the way it should be,[81] the ultimate project of the Ramsay Centre appeared to be to correct a fifty-year veering of humanities departments towards left-wing cultural relativism by directly imposing an alternative curriculum and pedagogy on top of them, helped by a large amount of philanthropic funding.

The deep irony is that the pre-emptively uncritical approach to the study of Western civilisation is antithetical to the Enlightenment commitment to scepticism and critique, which is central to the Western intellectual tradition. It also betrays a loss of faith in the robustness of the academic method that has led to so many of the political, intellectual and technological advances that the Ramsay Centre promoters celebrate. The academic method is based on the belief that all knowledge is contingent – meaning accepted until proven otherwise. In the words of historian Stefan Collini, 'the default condition of the scholar is one of intellectual dissatisfaction.'[82] For political philosopher Jonathan Rauch, the process of knowledge creation is a social one of disputation occurring according to agreed rules: 'Knowledge can only be made when it can be validated by others.'[83] The knowledge creation process, he argues, 'requires that propositions be contestable: subject to systematic, organised comparison and criticism from multiple points of view.'[84] To truly celebrate the Western intellectual tradition, we should put our trust in the robustness and self-correcting nature of this process of knowledge creation through contestation and validation according to agreed rules. That is the heart of the academic enterprise. To quote Rauch again, 'The reality-based community is explicitly based on self-correction.'[85] The Western intellectual tradition has veered many times into mistaken and destructive sidetracks, from the Inquisition, to eugenics, to leeching – but the method of critique, evidence and rational debate in time corrected these and other mistakes.

The movement towards critical theory and postmodernism that began in the 1960s is as much a part of the evolution of the Western intellectual tradition as quantum theory or monetarist economics. Like these, critical theory and postmodernism have been subject to rigorous debate and critique ever since, and many academics in the humanities and social sciences certainly do not see them as ascendant or particularly influential in current scholarship. That the followers of Allan Bloom see them as victorious, unchallenged and increasingly powerful in broader society is to subscribe to a bizarre version of Fukuyama's end of history thesis. Perhaps the strangest coda to the Ramsay Centre controversy is a March 2020 article written by Greg Sheridan, friend of Tony Abbott and supporter of the Ramsay Centre, which argues that the critical culture in the West that 'has mocked authority, glorified rebellion, sanctified the individual's quest for ever deeper self-realisation' has made societies such as Australia weaker than those based on Confucian principles which 'stress proper relations, family fidelity, respect for elders, respect for authority, personal morality and acting with some decorum. They esteem formal education, sober wisdom. You should respect and obey your parents, you should respect and generally obey your government'.[86] Was he implying that a replacement of our culture of critique and disagreement with the proper study of the Western canon would bring us closer to Confucian societies' respect and obedience?

After negotiations between ANU and the Ramsay Centre ended, negotiations began and then ended with the University of Sydney. Eventually agreement was reached with the University of Wollongong and the University of Queensland, both of which now offer a Bachelor of Western Civilisation. The terms of the agreement between the Ramsay Centre and the University of Queensland remain secret. Reviewing the *Sturm und Drang* of the Ramsay Centre episode, it is hard to escape the conclusion that the proponents of the Western civilisation concept were determined from the outset to provoke just the sort of response from humanities academics that they have been warning about. By forcing the discussion of Western civilisation down a Manichean path – 'anyone not with us is evidence for why we are necessary' – the terms on which Abbott shaped the issue precluded calm, reasoned debate. One wonders whether such people really believe that better policy and better education are delivered by the polarising language and tactics they seem to so enjoy deploying.

Freedom by Fiat

The controversies over the Ramsay Centre, the Ridd case and the Pavlou affair were closely watched by members of the federal government. Several entered the fray on the side of those attacking the universities involved, and notably no member of the government ventured into the debate urging calm or suggesting that the universities might have a case to make. No doubt prompted by the growing anger on the Treasury benches, in late 2018 education minister Dan Tehan commissioned a review of freedom of speech at Australian universities, to be chaired by former chief justice of Australia and chancellor of the University of Western Australia Robert French. The commission's comprehensive report, released in March 2019, found no evidence of a freedom of speech crisis on Australian university campuses, but after reviewing the situation relating to freedom of speech at universities in Australia, the United States, Canada, New Zealand and the United Kingdom, developed a 'model code' for the protection of freedom of speech on Australian campuses.[87] Several universities responded by altering their own academic freedom provisions to bring them closer to the French Model Code, while Universities Australia advised that its members would review their own policies to adopt the code, adapt its provisions or ensure its principles were reflected in their own practices. This, however, was not enough to calm the angst. In August 2020, Dan Tehan commissioned former Deakin University vice-chancellor Sally Walker to undertake a review to determine whether universities were sufficiently compliant with the French Model Code. The Walker Report, produced in December 2020, graded Australia's universities on whether they were 'fully aligned', 'mostly aligned', 'partly aligned' or 'not aligned' with the Model Code.[88]

Tehan's successor, Alan Tudge, warned soon after that 'if it becomes apparent that universities remain unable or unwilling to adopt the Model Code, I will examine all options available to the Government to enforce it – which may include legislation.'[89] The *Higher Education Support Act* was amended to ensure that clear references to academic freedom and freedom of speech were inserted. Tudge further flagged that universities would be required to report annually to government on their efforts to align their policies with the Model Code.[90] The irony was not lost on many. Goaded by a media and think tank campaign decrying a free speech crisis on campus, the government had commissioned a non-academic, who found no evidence of said crisis, to develop a model code to ensure universities' faithfulness to the oldest principle of academic practice. Another review followed, to hold Australia's universities up to scrutiny like naughty children in assessing how closely they adhered to this imposed model code. There was no thought given, in either French's or Walker's reviews, to whether those universities not 'fully aligned' with the model code were to a significant extent violating the practice of academic freedom or the principles of freedom of speech as a result. Neither was there any acknowledgement that the acts of imposing a model code, assessing universities' alignment with it, legislating alignment with it and threatening dire consequences if universities did not comply were themselves violations of the second principle of academic freedom, that universities will regulate their own behaviours in relation to academic practices. This is based on the (hitherto accepted) acknowledgement that governments and others outside of the academic profession do not have the expertise to assess what academics do, just as those outside of the medical profession are not qualified to assess the quality or integrity of what surgeons do.

What's next? Academic program reviews by think tanks? Curriculum design by politicians? Peer review by government panels? Ministerial review of the value of research? None of these suggestions is vaguely funny or hyperbolic because we have veered very close to each of them over the past five years. As publicly funded institutions, universities are subject to the tides of media commentary and public opinion, and the ever-tempting targets for increasingly draconian government regulation. The Morrison government's Job-ready Graduates Package showed how a government can manipulate levels of funding as a way of trying to change the number of students universities teach in disciplines the government has decided are not valuable to the economy. Governments' obsession with universities imparting students with the vocational skills needed by the economy as quickly and cheaply as possible is progressively stripping away the freedom of students and their teachers to explore their interests and deepen their understanding of multiple domains of knowledge.[91] On the research front, ministerial decisions to veto Australian Research Council funding to peer-reviewed and competitively assessed projects on opaque 'national interest' grounds suggests that political trumps academic judgement on what constitutes a worthy research project.[92] Meanwhile, the increasing pressure on universities to commercialise their research risks tying academic discovery increasingly to the needs of companies rather than allowing the free play of basic research that has so often in history produced the greatest advances in knowledge.[93] None of these threats to academic freedom by government action have raised even the smallest protest by the supposed partisans of academic freedom who rushed to the barricades over Ramsay, Ridd or Pavlou. It seems that the only serious threats to academic freedom come from the universities themselves.

A Culture Wars Memorial?

The Australian War Memorial stands as a permanent reminder of the folly and horror of war, but also as a tribute to the ideals for which so many have given their lives. To date, the culture wars over Australia's universities have claimed no casualties, and nor can we be certain they are over, but we should pause to reflect on them in the spirit of the twin messages that are central to the Australian War Memorial. The ideals that have animated the culture wars are sacred and central to Australian society: the unimpeded pursuit of knowledge for the broader benefit of Australian society, the robustness of its liberties and the enrichment of its civic culture. The folly of the culture wars lies in their hyper-partisan conduct, which itself threatens the academic ideals they are being fought over. Both sides are guilty of what Stefan Collini rightly sees as an unfortunate trend in academia and, it might be added, beyond academia:

> An unfortunate effect of much of the recent theoretical self-consciousness in academic disciplines has been to encourage the assumption that any scholar or critic is always working from within a *single* theory or paradigm: one has a favoured approach or methodology, an allegiance to a particular ism, and this, it is claimed, governs the type of work that can be done.[94]

A variation of this tendency, again apparent on both sides of the culture wars, is to begin with a particular political commitment, and assemble arguments, evidence and outrage in support of that commitment.

What the culture wars should remind us about, if we look in the right places, is the importance of maintaining the integrity of the academic enterprise. Sociologist Raewyn Connell describes the academic enterprise as the continual making and maintenance of a 'knowledge commons', a space in which academics are striving to 'create knowledge that can be trusted, used and reliably built on, in a continuing social process … In a university context, this means the body of knowledge (and the methods for making it) are held in trust by the research community as a whole'.[95] The founding agreement of the knowledge commons must be that no member can presume to know the whole truth about even a small area of knowledge, and for that reason should welcome the glorious diversity of any academic community. As Jonathan Rauch argues, the quintessential essence of any academic community is disagreement: 'Without pluralism and viewpoint diversity, transcending our biases is impossible, even in principle. Perfect objectivity will always elude us, but we come much closer if we follow the empirical rule by checking our views against others' different views, which of course is possible only where people disagree.'[96] But there have to be rules about *how* to disagree productively. It is here that both sides of the culture wars have let universities and society down badly. Both are guilty of what John Searle calls out as basic failures in argumentation: *argumentum ad hominem*, which dismisses an argument on the basis of who is making it; and the genetic fallacy, which assumes that because we disagree with where an argument originates, we can dismiss it altogether.[97] In academic life, as in the classroom, there is a recurring need to restate and agree upon the rules of the academic enterprise. Too often in Australian universities and beyond, these rules are assumed knowledge, but so frequently academic behaviour shows they are not.

Although many academics, students and supporters of Australia's universities have been frustrated, distressed and demoralised by the culture wars, with perspective we may see them as a welcome attraction of national attention to the role of universities in Australian life. In a neoliberal age, it was the culture wars that drew attention to the civic, social and political contribution of universities to the nation, beyond the relentless emphasis on the role of universities in creating economic value. But the culture wars also brought a more worrying message to Australia's universities: as public institutions, they will continue to be subject to the whims and concerns of the public and the governments of the day, as stimulated and buffered by self-interested think tanks and media organisations. In this context, the greatest challenge to the academic integrity of Australia's universities is a public and government motivated by partisan campaigns. Finding a powerful and compelling voice to speak back to these campaigns and concerns has to be a priority for Australia's universities.

5

Ambition

AUSTRALIA'S UNIVERSITIES HAVE developed a new ritual. Each now regularly hosts visits to its campuses by important people – government ministers, foreign officials, prominent philanthropists and businesspeople – and takes them immediately to its glimmering innovation and commercialisation hub. Each visitor is shown high-tech labs, creator spaces and co-creation initiatives with private industry, guided by a commentary explaining how the university is a force at the forefront of global technological innovation, dedicated to research commercialisation and central to meeting an array of global challenges, from pandemics and climate change to social cohesion. A big emphasis is placed on the university's partnerships – with global corporations, 'unicorns', tech start-ups, social entrepreneurs and major foundations – all of which have chosen it as the knowledge-creating secret sauce in their role of transforming the world for the better. In this ritual can be found Australian universities' new positioning in society, as institutions that are essential to Australia realising its innovative potential, avoiding economic stagnation, competing against the world's best, and creating a dynamic, innovative economy and workforce.

What gives these rituals their gravitas is the prevailing zeitgeist, repeated with endless variations by organisations such as the World Economic Forum, that a tsunami called the 'fourth industrial revolution' is poised to crash across the global economy, upending whole industries and hierarchies:

We are at the beginning of a global transformation that is characterised by the convergence of digital, physical and biological technologies ... This transformation – the fourth industrial revolution – is not defined by any particular set of emerging technologies themselves but rather by the transition to new systems that are being built on the infrastructure of the global revolution ... The fundamental and global nature of this revolution also poses new threats related to the disruptions it may cause – affecting labour markets and the future of work, income inequality, geopolitical security as well as social value systems and ethical frameworks.[1]

Anticipation of an impending era of technology-driven disruption has injected both ambition and anxiety into the national conversation about Australia's future. Governments at the national, state and local levels have adopted the optimistic mantra of innovation, creativity and a technology enabled future as electorally successful policy frameworks. The cultural prominence of firms such as Google, Facebook and Amazon, and the posturing of their multi-billionaire founders, has embedded hopes of the transformative potential of information technology deep within Australian society. But as countries such as the United States, Israel and China position themselves at the forefront of the global innovation revolution, the question nags constantly in Australian minds: will this revolution be the next phase in Australia's prosperity or will Australia be left to quietly decline in its wake?

Australia's universities have positioned themselves as an essential ingredient in this country's ability to rise to the challenge of the fourth industrial revolution. The twin imperatives driving this positioning are the need to further underwrite their financial viability in an era of rising costs and stagnant public funding, and the opportunity for them to demonstrate their public usefulness in addressing a major imperative confronting the nation. It's inevitable that Australian universities will be at the centre of the new knowledge economy agenda, as the rise of international education and the internationalisation of research has put them at the heart of the emergence of a global knowledge industry, recognised and now regulated under the General Agreement on Trade in Services.[2] The global knowledge industry is by nature highly competitive – for resources, talent, prestige and recognition – bringing new competitive logics into the Australian higher education sector which are reshaping it profoundly. Australia's universities need to respond to two layers of competition: a national science and higher education policy framework, increasingly oriented around research output accountability and commercialisation imperatives; and a global sectorial innovation system, driven by the relentless contest for technological and commercial advantage, and increasingly shaped by geopolitical competition over technology and innovation.[3] The shift in Australian universities' missions and operations has been profound, as 'universities … have had to "learn to compete" due to the transformation of universities and higher education institutions to become knowledge businesses, instead of societal institutions providing public services'.[4] They have been remarkably successful in adapting to the new logic as 'present-day universities are more capable and more inclined to position themselves in competitive processes for resources, reputation and talent, and to formulate organisational strategies to defend and improve their competitive position'.[5] Adding to the competitive pressures has been the emergence and entrenching of global university rankings systems, which expose universities to structured, quantifiable comparisons across variables that purport to measure university quality.

The transposing of ambition and competition to the centre of Australian universities' roles in Australian life is fraught with consequences. It has undoubtedly intensified competition over 'vertical differentiation' – the imperative to distinguish universities on a hierarchic scale of quality and prestige – while decreasing, if not erasing, the tendency towards 'horizontal competition' – differentiating between universities by function, focus and mission – leading to what former University of Melbourne vice-chancellor Glyn Davis identified as a lack of variety within Australia's higher education sector.[6] It may also be generating a negative dynamic: as universities are pulled deeper into national ambitions for innovation, productivity and economic success, society becomes more critical and less satisfied that they are adequately playing those roles. There is a danger that in positioning themselves as central to the knowledge economy, universities could end up becoming the scapegoats for the economy's failures to compete. The innovation and commercialisation imperative has also stirred up a very old debate in Australia, as in other societies, over the purpose of the university as an institution producing knowledge for its own sake or for instrumental ends. This debate has its roots in the nineteenth century, when opinion divided over whether universities' purpose was to curate and produce a '"pure" or "immaculate" conception of knowledge and education for its own sake' or to be dedicated to 'the instrumental or utilitarian ethos, focused on the creation and dissemination of useful knowledge and the training of students with useful skills'.[7] In Germany, France, England and the United States, this distinction led to the creation of differentiated 'classical' and 'technical' universities, before the Dutch and Scottish universities pioneered a model combining classical education and professional training that spread to Europe, North America and Australia.[8] But recent debates over Australian universities' innovation and commercialisation imperatives have reignited old divisions over whether universities should be dedicated to the pursuit of knowledge for its own sake or for utilitarian ends.

Conjuring the Knowledge Economy

The notion of a 'knowledge economy' was popularised by futurist Peter Drucker in his 1969 book, *The Age of Discontinuity*, which described a future where the crucial inputs for economic success would not be the finance, resources, energy and manufactures that had driven the post–World War II boom, but advances in human understanding.[9] As the developed economies succumbed to a prolonged recession following the 1973 oil shock, booming economies such as Japan – which appeared to be outcompeting established industrial powers through clever innovations – seemed to add credence to Drucker's predictions. The Australian Labor Party took to the 1983 election a separate, dedicated science and technology policy. It observed that countries with the greatest increases in gross national product since 1955 had invested in the education of their people, and those with high export earnings had benefited from high levels of 'intellectual skills' among their populations. Labor pledged to reform the economy to generate more wealth with high-tech industry, committing to increase the Australian Research Grants Commission's funding by 10 per cent.[10] Education minister John Dawkins saw that increasing the number of Australians with higher education qualifications would be essential to Australia building a dynamic economy. Today, he believes that Australia's higher proportion of university graduates that flowed from the Dawkins reforms is a significant and unacknowledged part of the success of the Hawke–Keating reforms which generated three decades of economic expansion.[11] Those economic reforms soon informed a new imperative that developed from the late 1980s, which encouraged governments to foster the development of 'national innovation systems'.[12] Here was an economic paradigm to aim for after a decade of recession and stagflation. The end of the Cold War saw concern with national economic competitiveness replace a focus on national security, bringing greater attention to the commercial returns from government funding of university research.[13] As the 1990s progressed, and new technologies such as the internet, email and mobile phones began transforming society and the economy, innovation centres such as Boston's Route 128 and California's Silicon Valley captured the imagination of politicians and the public alike. A new era of techno-optimism and innovation ambition was dawning.

The new era also brought attention to the contribution of Massachusetts Institute of Technology (MIT) to the Route 128 innovation story and Stanford University's pivotal role in Silicon Valley. Australia's universities, recently ushered towards corporatisation by the Dawkins reforms, began to imagine similar roles for themselves within Australia's national innovation system. Like universities around the world, they responded by willingly taking on a role as crucial actors in Australia's knowledge economy, thereby adding a third mission to their traditional dual purposes of teaching and research.[14] University mission statements were soon peppered with references to their contribution to Australia's innovation and productivity, regional development and solving societal challenges. As they stepped into this role, it became clear that a major difference between Australia's universities and exemplars such as MIT and Stanford was the level of research funding received. Both MIT and Stanford, along with a handful of other American universities, had received hundreds of millions of dollars in research funding from the US government to conduct research considered vital to national security. Political scientist Linda Weiss describes a complex process through which US defence and intelligence agencies funded university research and invested in research commercialisation that would be both commercially useful and valuable in developing defence and intelligence capabilities.[15] In Australia, it didn't take long for a direct link to be drawn between universities' ability to contribute to Australia's innovation success and the amount of research funding they received from the government.

It became a common theme in university lobbying: Australia's universities had stepped up and were producing great innovations that were contributing to the sophistication and dynamism of the economy, but unless the Australian government arrested the decline or stagnation in research and development funding, Australia would fall behind competitor economies in innovation-driven development.[16] It seems the connection between research funding and national innovation and competitiveness had started to filter through to public opinion by the turn of the century. Former education minister Brendan Nelson recalls Prime Minister John Howard picking up on concerns in focus group discussions about Australia's research and innovation competitiveness in the late 1990s, leading him to commission work on the potential and financing of Australia's research ecosystem.[17] The Howard government held a National Innovation Summit in February 2000, the results of which contributed to the launch of the Backing Australia's Ability policy in January 2001. In committing the government to a $2.9-billion increase in research funding over five years, the policy picked out most of the salient elements identified in discussions of national innovation systems: university research; research infrastructure; information technology and biotechnology centres of excellence; university-business R&D collaboration; and increasing the nation's science and technology education levels. In the fore-word to the policy statement, Howard wrote,

> The Government believes that the strategy marks a significant step in harnessing the collective talent, energy and resources of all those dedicated to securing Australia's economic future, both within and outside Government. It represents a commitment to pursue excellence in research, science and technology, to build an even more highly skilled workforce and increase opportunities for the commercialisation of new ideas – in essence it is about backing Australia's ability.[18]

There is considerable evidence that universities' framing of their central role in Australia's knowledge economy future has gained traction. As the COVID-19 pandemic hit in 2020, governments closed borders and enforced lockdowns, shuttering businesses and throwing the Australian economy into hibernation. It was an economic shock the likes of which had never been seen nor envisaged. As minds turned to the revival of a shattered economy beyond the pandemic, universities were regularly conjured as central to Australia's economic reconstruction. The chancellor of the University of Sydney was one of many who made the analogy with the postwar boom, recalling 'the role that higher education played in the reconstruction of the Australian economy after World War II. And it's easy to see the parallels with our current situation … Universities are an economic powerhouse, boosting the economy in times of trouble, something that governments have known in the past and resonates with us now.'[19] Education minister

Dan Tehan agreed, arguing, 'research will be essential to help power Australia's coronavirus recovery. The productive capacity of our nation will rely on educated workers, able to access innovation and research, to drive opportunity.'[20] Universities were repeatedly held up as pivotal institutions in the economy as a whole, as well as for regional communities and economies. For those who saw a critical role for universities in Australia's post-pandemic recovery, the government's lack of support for higher education during the pandemic was both inexplicable and unforgiveable.[21]

A variation on this theme was the emphasis placed on universities as central to Australia's response to significant challenges. There was no shortage of advocates and acknowledgements of the crucial contributions made by university expertise to Australia's response to the coronavirus pandemic.[22] Other national priorities are also called out as requiring Australia's universities: renewable energy; defence capabilities; outer-space capacity; artificial intelligence; medical research; robotics. Some argued that universities were playing a core role in helping the country find its future in Asia; or that they were vital for building the country's self-sufficiency.[23] Often the stories of university successes came from the universities themselves, but there was plenty of evidence that they had become firmly established in Australians' imaginations about the role of higher education in the country's economic future.

The counterpart to techno-optimism is techno-pessimism, an anxiety that ultimately Australia might not have what it takes to succeed in the knowledge economy and will fall further and further behind. Driving much of this techno-pessimism is the social Darwinism that imbues much of the contemporary discussion about the knowledge economy, implying that those firms and nations that are first to breach the innovation frontier will reap huge gains, while those not innovating constantly will be technology's price-takers.[24] As early as 1980, a meeting of the OECD declared a public crisis of confidence in the value of higher education in achieving national economic objectives or supplying an appropriate workforce.[25] More recently, concerns have been voiced that 'Australia has enjoyed complacent prosperity, we have done very well by exploiting our natural resource endowments and decade after decade of high population growth driving property and building development', but pointing out that these advantages remove the incentive to invest in innovation via the knowledge economy.[26] Different measures are found to illustrate how far behind the innovation frontier Australia is falling: 'Measured by the research intensity of our exports, Australia's "economic complexity" ranks between Kazakhstan and Lebanon.'[27] In the case of quantum computing – one of the 'defining technologies of the twenty-first century', according to one specialist – 'estimates prior to 2015 placed Australia sixth in the world for sovereign level investment into quantum technology. As of 2021, we have fallen to last place.'[28] As techno-pessimism takes hold, inevitably attention falls on universities as key players in Australia's knowledge economy. Compared to other countries, Australia's universities have been accused of being insufficiently innovative in driving the digital revolution in Australia.[29] The pandemic further heightened fears of the nation falling behind the knowledge frontier, as financial challenges and an exhausted academic workforce cut into universities' productivity. Commentators wonder about

Australian universities' ability to maintain their positioning in the global rankings and preserve the country's future research capability in the face of the pandemic and unsympathetic government policy settings.[30] This concern with positioning in the global rankings seems to have been a timeless one, but actually the obsession with rankings is a recent yet momentous development in how we think about our universities.

It's a Long Way to the Top

Early in the twenty-first century, a new force emerged that would reshape how Australians viewed their universities. Unasked-for and unforeseen, the world's universities found themselves compared against each other and listed according to league tables that purported to provide objective measures of the relative quality of universities in hundreds of countries. Almost overnight, a university in Ghana could be compared to one in Guyana; a campus in Paris with one in Pretoria; a Columbia business degree with a business degree from Colombia. The idea of comparing and ranking universities was first popularised by James McKeen Cattell, who compiled a ranking of American colleges and universities in 1906. It would take almost a century before the idea of rankings went global.

In 2003, China's Shanghai Jiao Tong University published a global ranking of universities based around a common and transparent methodology of comparison, in time known as the Academic Ranking of World Universities (ARWU). A year later, *Times Higher Education* (THE) published its own ranking of universities around the world, based on a different methodology of comparison. A third authoritative ranking emerged soon after with the Quacquarelli Symonds (QS) league table of global universities, using yet another approach for comparing and ranking universities. The timing of the emergence of the 'big three' university rankings was impeccable, coinciding with the expansion of university education in developed nations and the rise of international education more generally. Global rankings emerged as an easy guide to higher education just as the sector was becoming rapidly more complex, competitive and internationalised.[31]

The public impact of global university rankings has outgrown their originators' wildest expectations, leading them to refine and extend their frameworks. Now there are rankings of disciplines, researchers, graduate outcomes and social impact. Within universities, these global rankings are widely criticised and reviled, but such is their influence on both public and academic perceptions that no university on earth can afford not to play the rankings game. These three self-appointed appraisers of academic quality have changed the relationship between universities and societies forever; in the words of Simon Marginson, 'now the rankings genie is out of the bottle, it will always be with us.'[32]

Global university rankings tap into a public fascination with league tables. Each year the ARWU, THE and QS rankings are released with a blaze of publicity and duly accorded blanket coverage in the Australian media. Universities' publicity campaigns coalesce around them, with each finding a way to position itself favourably in one aspect of one of the rankings. Students and their parents follow suit, making choices and waxing superior on the basis of some facet of their chosen university's apparent eminence.

Rankings have become absorbed into considerations of higher education policy as well, with governments formulating plans on the perceived strengths and weaknesses of their higher education sector based on the findings of one Chinese and two British surveys. China has allocated billions of dollars to its university sector to compete with America's Ivy League; Russia, India, Japan, Taiwan, Singapore, Malaysia, Vietnam and others have determined their international education policies based around promoting some of their universities in the global rankings. By capturing the official imagination, 'within national systems the rankings have prompted the desire for more and higher-ranked universities, both as symbols of national achievement and prestige, and supposedly, as engines of the knowledge economy'.[33]

Similar pressures guide government planning in Australia also. The South Australian and Western Australian state governments have toyed with the idea of merging some of their universities to develop the scale to promote them in the global rankings.[34] Studies have showed that the global university rankings significantly affect trade, immigration, student flows, academic hiring, philanthropic support, commercial partnerships, tuition fees and the tenure and pay of vice-chancellors.[35] Rankings are increasingly important in student choices of where they will study, particularly for international students. With a greater than 50 per cent increase in the number of students travelling abroad to attend university since 2000, the impact of global rankings on their choices ultimately has a major effect on the revenue of universities.

The emergence and outsized influence of the global rankings has fundamentally reframed the positioning of universities in Australian life. Marginson observes that they are 'perhaps the decisive move in norming higher education as a global market.'[36] The rankings' capture of public and government attention has introduced a much sharper element of competition between universities. Studies show that the imperative of maintaining and improving their positioning in the global rankings now plays a major role in shaping the strategies of universities in Australia and around the world.[37]

But despite presenting themselves as objective and value-neutral, the global rankings are shot through with value judgements and cultural biases: 'Ranking exposes universities in every nation to structured global competition that operates on terms that favour some universities and countries, and disadvantage others.'[38] When broken down into their constituent elements, it is clear that the global rankings conform to a circular logic: their measures are set by a predetermined conception of what a good university looks like, and the data they collect confirms their predispositions by ranking highly the universities their preconceptions were based on. As determined by the rankings' measurement criteria, the world's best universities are large, research-intensive comprehensive institutions that are particularly strong in science, technology, engineering and medicine (STEM), and conduct their research and teaching in English. The rankings privilege research performance over teaching quality and other elements of university life, largely because (according to the rankings agencies) research data are more directly comparable than teaching or other data on university quality. The effects on university operations are important. The privileging of research drives both institutional and individual preferences and resource allocations. Studies show that orienting university strategy around the global rankings has negative effects on gender equity and the casualisation of the academic workforce, and increases stress and mental illness in the academic workforce.[39] The rankings reinforce existing hierarchies in higher education, with higher-ranked, more renowned universities attracting the best academic talent, students and resources, while smaller, lower-ranked universities that teach and research in languages other than English struggle to compete.

All three agencies behind the major global rankings have built substantial businesses around the runaway success of their rankings, offering consulting, software, conferences and other services to universities that wish to improve their positioning. They are confident enough in their influence to make statements such as THE's claim to be 'setting the agenda in higher education'.[40] The rankings are also closely tied into the other major oligopoly built on the globalisation of higher education: journal publishing. Nearly half of all academic papers published are circulated in journals produced by three publishers: Elsevier, Springer Nature and Wiley-Blackwell. Elsevier also runs one of the major citation databases that feed the rankings analysis, which studies have found significantly weights its citation methodology to favour papers published in Elsevier journals.[41] So choosing the 'right' journal to publish academic papers in can have a discernible effect on a university's rankings. It also means that academics outside of North America and Britain face pressure to publish their work in English and on topics that are deemed 'relevant' to the editors of the top journals, who themselves are most likely to be employed at highly ranked universities. The rankings have further reinforced the status of higher education as a prestige good, allowing higher-ranked universities to charge higher prices for admission, enabling them to invest more in the activities and capabilities that will further boost their ranking.

Many of Australia's universities have benefited from the global rankings. As the Group of Eight likes to point out, Australia has more universities in the global top 100 than any other nation other than the United States and the United Kingdom. The ability to use their positioning in the rankings to attract large numbers of international students has allowed the 'big five' Australian universities (Sydney, Melbourne, Monash, New South Wales and Queensland) each to generate annual revenues of over $2 billion, and to steadily climb the rankings through their investments in STEM research and infrastructure.[42] Although there are dire predictions about the impact of the pandemic lockdowns on Australian universities' rankings, they continued to rate highly in the 2020, 2021 and 2022 league tables.[43] Yet despite regular reporting of their universities' enhanced standings on global scales, there are few signs that ordinary Australians regard this with a sense of pride – pride in ranking highly in global competitions appears to be something Australians reserve for sporting teams and athletes. When university rankings are mentioned, it tends to be for negative effect, such as pointing out their wealth and privilege, and the undeserving nature of their pleas for more public money.[44] Australia's universities are also accused of chasing rankings success over other values, such as student experience, suggesting that their position in the global rankings is a solipsistic obsession important to universities but not to broader

Australian society.[45] But this hasn't stopped Australian universities from featuring their high standing in their marketing and recruitment materials.

Going Commercial

In the context of optimism and anxiety about Australia's performance in the knowledge economy, universities soon came to be judged against another comparative international benchmark: their success in commercialising their research. Once again, overseas universities such as Cambridge and Stanford were held up as exemplars which Australia's universities were expected to match. Many universities took it as a 'third mission' to be added to their traditional academic pursuits.[46] External encouragement of university research commercialisation came from government, with its own imperatives to promote the development of the knowledge economy as well as to find additional non-public revenue for higher education; and from corporations looking to widen their knowledge bases and externalise their research and development operations.[47] Advocates of research commercialisation talked up the need to demonstrate the public value of university research, the opportunity to bolster public trust in science, and the ability to demonstrate the public return on the investment of taxpayers' money in university research.[48]

However, when compared to success stories from overseas, Australia's universities are judged to be falling short in the research commercialisation race:

In the past 15 years there have been more than 60 reports on Australia's national innovation system. They all broadly reach the same finding: Australia suffers from a failure to turn high levels of public research into commercial outcomes, has low levels of business research and development, lacks specialist business services and finance supports, and has limited connections into global supply chains to scale new businesses with global potential.[49]

International rankings on research commercialisation were much less flattering than the rankings of universities, finding that 'Australia currently ranks last in the OECD for business collaboration on innovation with higher education or government institutions'.[50] Diagnoses abound on why Australia lags in commercialisation, but most return to an insufficiently entrepreneurial culture in its universities: 'due to a poor commercialisation process and little incentive for academics to unlock their research there are simply not enough successful spin-out businesses from our universities in proportion to the R&D spent.'[51] There has been much discussion of the dramatically named 'valley of death' between universities' research breakthroughs and the conversion of those into commercially viable products. Inevitably, explanations converge on some form of market failure, suggesting a role for governments in ensuring both universities and business are sufficiently incentivised to come together to commercialise university research.[52]

The value of academic research in promoting national interests was amply demonstrated during World War II, with a steady stream of research breakthroughs providing the Allies with the decisive advantage over the Axis powers: nuclear fission; radar; encryption and decryption. A continuing national interest in funding university research was recognised by Vannevar Bush, a former MIT Dean of Engineering and presidential science adviser, in his 1945 report to President Roosevelt, *Science, The Endless Frontier*.[53] Bush, the founder of the company Raytheon and inventor of a string of patents, firmly believed that while research should be funded from the public purse, university academics should be free to pursue their inquiries free of government instruction or directives. This would be the approach to university research funding adopted by most Western governments during the 1950s, '60s and '70s.[54] But as public finances tightened in the 1970s and university-government relations became testier, governments became less trusting that academic self-governing processes, such as peer review, would ensure taxpayers' money was well spent. By the late 1970s, governments were tying research funding to certain national priorities and using competition for scarce research funding to ensure academics were researching what the nation believed it needed. The link between 'useful' research and commercial outcomes was created by the passage of the *Bayh-Dole Act* through the United States Congress in 1980, providing incentives for universities to patent inventions flowing from publicly funded research by allowing universities and academics to keep the commercial proceeds of their marketable inventions. The rest of the OECD followed suit shortly after, placing commercialisation of research as a key indicator of university success and service of the national interest.[55] The concurrent success of several biotechnology companies in commercialising early research results in genetic engineering served as a clear model for the commercialisation of other areas of science.[56]

Seeing an opportunity to demonstrate the public benefit of their existence and activities, Australian universities and research institutes such as the CSIRO signed on to the commercialisation imperative, and were soon being compared according to the number of successful start-up companies their graduates had founded.[57] Soon they were touting a range of made-in-Australia commercial successes, from wi-fi to the bionic ear to in-vitro fertilisation. Many universities saw commercial partnerships, patents and royalties as a new form of funding independent of the taxpayer, prompting them to 'reshape their research orientations and structures by partnering with private sector corporations, seeking grants from external funding bodies, patenting discoveries, providing research-based advisory services and … commercialising research outputs, perhaps by creating spin-off companies'.[58] A common move was to create a subsidiary company within the university to provide academics with access to business development expertise and even small amounts of venture capital. Commercial revenue generation and the registering of patents became the new metrics of research success, both for individual academics and for universities. Research management within universities has begun to shift from 'supporting individual autonomous researchers to fostering, managing and evaluating research teams that can produce commercialisable research'.[59]

The increasing precarity of the academic workforce, with large numbers of scientists on short-term contracts tied to external research funding, has internalised commercial research imperatives across whole fields of research. Universities are increasingly having to mediate the tension between the academic ideal of self-directed exploratory research and the external imperatives of directed, exploitable research. Many try to manage the tension with an 'ambidextrous' approach, which seeks to encourage and enable both self-directed and commercially oriented academic research.[60] Internal research funding schemes have been reshaped along competitive lines, with both their logics and their criteria replicating external competitive funding. Within these new competitive environments, universities and individuals have become more strategic, reshaping their internal processes and external positioning to best succeed and outcompete their rivals.[61]

Unsurprisingly, the commercialisation imperative is controversial within Australia's universities, with some embracing it as an opportunity and others viewing it as a threat to the integrity of the academic calling. There is scepticism that even the exemplars of commercialisation, such as Stanford and Hebrew University, derive a significant proportion of their operating revenues from patents and spin-offs. Some argue that commercial imperatives are shifting academic research from serving the public interest to benefiting private interests, potentially undermining public trust in the impartiality of science; and that by directing research towards particular ends, the commercialisation imperative compromises academic autonomy, creativity and innovation.[62] The push for commercialisable discoveries, it is claimed, is increasing cases of researcher bias and fraud, while restricting access to the full range of scientific knowledge necessary for further breakthroughs.[63]

Confidentially, many scientists will relate stories of private sector companies buying proprietary rights to particular discoveries and then suppressing them in order to preserve the commercial advantage of their existing products. In this environment, the influence of academic and disciplinary integrity practices becomes crucial. On the other side of the debate are those who claim that 'basic research' is being too fetishised, and that basic and directed research can coexist quite comfortably. Those asserting the superiority of basic research are accused of making an elitist claim to its superiority to somewhat grubby, compromised applied research; revisiting the sublime–mundane duality that underpins many attitudes towards universities and their purpose.[64] Others scoff at the idea of 'pure' self-directed research, arguing that all academic inquiry is inspired and constrained by current intellectual fashions anyway.[65]

Human Capital

Universities are cast as having dual roles in the knowledge economy: helping to create the new technologies and industries of the future; and training the workforce with the increasingly sophisticated skills needed to operate successfully in the fourth industrial revolution. An early connection between university education and building the workforce skills for the knowledge economy was made by the OECD, which included a chapter on 'Education and Human Capital' in its 1987 report 'Structural Adjustment and Economic Performance', arguing that a 'basic policy goal' of education was 'to increase the productivity of human resources'.[66] A series of studies followed, showing strong correlations between educational attainment, income and economic growth rates.[67] The human capital argument was enthusiastically seized on by both sides of politics in Australia as demonstrating the public and private benefits of higher education; these arguments were influential at the individual level also, driving steady increases in the participation rates in higher education in Australia from the mid-1980s.[68] Once again, there were optimistic and pessimistic takes on Australia's human capital development. The former focused on the growth of the services sector and the globalisation of talent and opportunities; the latter on whether Australia's higher education sector was up to building the human capital the country needed to succeed in the knowledge economy.

The release of Australia's first Intergenerational Report by Treasurer Peter Costello in 2002 focused further attention on Australia's long-term demographic challenges and their likely effects on the country's long-term prosperity and productivity.[69] The regular release of subsequent Intergenerational Reports continued to focus attention on the future adequacy of the Australian workforce, reinforcing a pessimistic tone on whether Australia had what it took to succeed in the knowledge economy. Predictions of technology-driven disruption raised anxiety among employers and workers alike about whether they would be able to access the skills needed to succeed in the fourth industrial revolution: 'Digital disruption is rapidly breaking down long-established business models and blurring lines between companies and industries. In doing so it alters organisational processes and traditional ways of operating and delivering goods and services; it also changes workforce needs, knowledge, skills and capabilities.'[70] Demographic analysis suggested the growth in the supply and sophistication of the Australian workforce would slow significantly as the baby boom and the increased participation of women in the workforce flowed through, leaving the country struggling to find the skilled workers it would need: 'At a time when technological change will be very rapid and Australia will need to be shifting to new energy sources and new forms of energy efficient infrastructure, a fairly substantial fall in numbers of young skilled workers seems a very risky situation.'[71]

Concerns over skills shortages reached new levels as Australia's borders shut during the COVID-19 pandemic. Where 2019 had seen 250,000 people added to the Australian population, the year to March 2021 saw a net reduction of 95,000, creating a cumulative migration shortfall of 375,000 during the first year of the pandemic. Anecdotes of skills shortages and their drag on the country's economy became commonplace in 2021 and 2022, becoming a major imperative for governments and prompting the new Labor government to hold a Jobs and Skills Summit in September 2022.

Attention turned to universities and whether, despite educating greater proportions of each generation of Australians, they were training them in the skills the economy needed. Data was produced showing significant mismatches between university graduates' qualifications and the necessary skills, particularly in technology: 'despite the information revolution, only 3 per cent of domestic graduates have an information technology qualification, down from 6 per cent in the early 2000s.'[72] Universities' willingly assumed role in the knowledge economy became a stick for critics to beat them with, as well as generating accusations that Australian university degrees are boutique and irrelevant to the needs of their graduates.[73] A government-commissioned review of Australia's workforce skills needs by former vice-chancellors Peter Dawkins and Martin Bean found that 'while Australia is sixth on the World Economic Forum's ranking of tertiary education attainment, it drops to tenth for business relevance and twelfth for the supply of business relevant skills'.[74] An increasing clamour arose, urging the government to force universities to teach students skills needed in the economy, and to prioritise international students intending to study in fields needed by the Australian economy. New attention fell on the employability of graduates from different universities, and the average salary levels of graduates from different universities.

By mid-2020, both government and Opposition had endorsed the view that a prime rationale for Australia's universities was to ensure the country had adequate numbers of workers with the appropriate skills to ensure the economy's productivity and prosperity. Education minister Dan Tehan capitalised on the sentiment that universities needed to be refocused on educating in the areas the economy needed: more engineers, computer programmers and nurses; fewer lawyers, accountants and humanities graduates. In the most significant reform to higher education in Australia since the introduction of the demand-driven system by his predecessor Julia Gillard, Tehan's Job-ready Graduates Package aimed to shift the proportions of students studying what were seen as less useful degrees towards those seen as more useful by altering considerably the cost of different degrees. The desired degrees would become cheaper, the superfluous ones dearer. Relying on some highly questionable costings provided by Deloitte Access Economics, the Tehan reforms had the perverse effect of making certain 'useful' degrees – such as in the sciences – uneconomic for universities to teach, while enabling them to make money on degrees called out as useless. The package passed the parliament in late 2020, leaving universities to ponder how they would teach now-uneconomic degrees, and how they would cope with the surge in applications arising from the demographic bubble caused by the Howard government's payment of 'baby bonuses' in the early 2000s. Initial enrolment data showed that price was a poor motivator of student choice when compared to intrinsic interest or aptitude.[75] Perhaps most interesting was the vocal opposition to Tehan's conception of universities as 'skills factories' from academics, students and members of the public, arguing for the value of a broad education for both employment and career reasons and for broader social enrichment reasons.[76]

Competition – Within Limits

For Australia's universities not to have embraced the new logic of competition heralded by the knowledge economy, global rankings, commercialisation and the focus on human capital would have condemned them to irrelevance. Arguably they have responded highly effectively to these competitive logics, even if broader Australian society seems determined to give them little credit and takes no pride in their successes. Despite doomsayers arguing that technology driven disruption will undermine traditional universities' 'business models', they responded with creativity and innovation to the lockdowns that forced all classes online, along with a range of other teaching innovations. Stories of delivering experiment kits and musical instruments to students in lockdown are common in most of Australia's universities, but little known outside them.

However, Australia's universities need to remain vigilant that the logic of competition, rankings, commercialisation and human capital building, if allowed to exercise free rein, could distort the basic mission of our higher education institutions. Competition has always played a productive role in academic research – but so has collaboration. Sharing one's discoveries, holding them up to scepticism and peer review, and engaging in free and productive debate are practices that have underpinned the productivity and integrity of universities for centuries. In investing in our universities' competitive capabilities, we must never lose sight of these fundamental collaboration-based practices, nor compromise them in the name of temporary advantage. There is strong and encouraging evidence that academics and universities are alive to cases where the logic of competition and ranking is having perverse effects on academic life. In 2005, physicist Jorge Hirsch proposed the 'h-index', as a way of measuring the productivity and impact of academic researchers by combining the number of papers an academic has published and the number of citations received. Although widely used, the h-index also began to attract criticism for its pernicious effects on innovation, creativity and academics' willingness to challenge highly-cited concepts. In April

2015, the journal *Nature* called attention to the distorting effects of bibliometric measures such as the h-index, and proposed the Leiden Manifesto for Research Metrics, which set out ten principles for research evaluation that would avoid the distorting effects of simplistic metrics.[77] The growing influence of the Leiden Manifesto shows universities and academics playing their self-regulatory roles in relation to externally imposed measurements. Competition is good only when it is healthy and respectful of the academic ecosystem.

6

Privilege

PHOEBE AND CONNOR are uni students. Phoebe is in her second year of a Bachelor of Biomedicine. She has an active social and sports life and is quite involved in university politics, but needs to keep her weighted average mark high in order to get into the country's best medical school. Luckily her residential college provides extra tutoring and has hired someone who is also a part-time demonstrator in some of Phoebe's lab classes. She's also got the advantage that her parents, who met at her college thirty years ago, are both doctors living not too far away in the leafy eastern suburbs of the state's capital city. Connor is a third year in a Bachelor of Health Sciences (Health and Lifestyle) degree. He's supporting himself, his partner and their one-year-old twins by working three days a week for a local landscaping business in the regional city they live in. He can do his classes during the other two days. He's had to give up playing rugby league because he can't afford to get injured and doesn't have the time anyway. Being the first person from his family to go to uni, he cops a fair bit of questioning about why he's kept studying. His dad keeps sending him newspaper articles that argue that most uni degrees aren't worth the paper they're printed on.[1] But Connor isn't a quitter. He knows there will always be work in the growing number of health centres and aged care homes in that part of the country. And he knows that what separates the managers from the workers is a uni degree.

Connor's access to university is governed by the same regulations and requirements as Phoebe's. They will both pay the same amount for their degrees once they've graduated and are earning over a certain income threshold. But that's where their commonalities end. Connor would never have contemplated going to Phoebe's university, and had he applied would not have had a high enough entry score. Phoebe has never heard of Connor's university and wouldn't have applied even if she had known of it. Connor's degree will likely earn him over $1 million more than his mates, who stopped at the higher school certificate (HSC), over the course of his career; Phoebe's degrees will allow her to earn many multiple times what Connor earns.

Connor and Phoebe are two among millions of Australians for whom going to university is a portal to professional employment and standing, career choice and security, and social advancement. In Australia, as in many other countries, 'higher education provides a sophisticated set of social technologies for transforming human personality and capability and helping people to transform themselves'. In doing so, according to Simon Marginson, it 'provides an opportunity structure … crucial to the health of its societies. Without higher education, the uneven distribution of wealth and power alone would shape the life possibilities of young people, setting decisive limits on their fate.'[2] But he argues, higher education is also 'a society-wide system of social allocation and selection.'[3] Connor's and Phoebe's two very different experiences of university in today's Australia illustrate the two contradictory logics of higher education in this country that Marginson describes. On the one hand, university will be an enabler of opportunity and social mobility for both young people, providing them with opportunities and advantages they would never have had if they had chosen not to attend. But Phoebe brought to her university years advantages that Connor never had: a private school education, a wealthy inner-city upbringing, social confidence and a sense of belonging to the best colleges and universities. Despite an expansion of access to greater proportions of Australian society over the past generation, universities remain exclusive institutions, their prestige and social value determined by whom they choose to exclude. This has resulted in the paradox that while the Australian higher education sector has become more inclusive, it has also become a more intense creator of hierarchy and privilege in Australian society. Connor's university may end up distinguishing him from his mates who stopped with the HSC, but Phoebe's university will ensure that the social space between her and Connor widens.

Privilege for All?

For much of their first century, Australian universities were unashamedly places of social privilege. Founded for the purpose of training a cultivated elite to lead the colonies, there was one university for each state capital, providing admission to a very small proportion of the state's population. Although the fees to attend university were modest, the ability to pay them and to support oneself through years of study meant that higher education was largely the preserve of the wealthy social elite. As in Britain, Australia's universities required applicants to sit a university-set matriculation examination, for which candidates would need years of specific preparation. Overwhelmingly, it was the private grammar schools that provided the appropriate preparations for the matriculation exams. As successive generations attended Australia's universities, sons and daughters tended to attend the same universities and colleges, and study the same degrees, as their parents had. Before World War II, less than 0.2 per cent of the Australian population held a university qualification. But during this time, attending university was by no means the only route to social mobility and distinction. There were a range of professions, such as engineering, architecture, pharmacy and teaching, that were highly esteemed in society but did not require a university qualification. University men and women were respected in broader society as a slightly exotic species, but they were only one among the myriad social distinctions of twentieth-century Australian life.

The experience of World War II changed this as it did so many aspects of Australian society. More than ever before, this had been a war of technologies and knowledge, giving decisive advantages to those countries with the brains to complement their brawn. Although Australia had barely been physically touched by the conflict, the war had caused an epochal upheaval in Australian leaders' understandings of what Australian society would need to do to protect itself and prosper in the new world created in the aftermath of the conflagration. Australia would need a comprehensive program of postwar 'reconstruction', building its economy, society and institutions anew in order to make its way amid the technology-driven uncertainties in the years ahead.[4] An immediate challenge for the Labor government at the end of the war was how to integrate tens of thousands of servicemen and servicewomen back into Australian life. Following the United States and other allies, Australia introduced a Commonwealth Reconstruction Training Scheme (CRTS), providing scholarships and university access for people returning from the war. The rationale was to use higher education to support the morale and employment prospects of returned service personnel while at the same time creating a labour force with the technical capabilities to build the new postwar economy.[5] It was a decisive moment in broadening participation in the Australian university sector. By 1949, university attendance in Australia had tripled. 'From then on,' observes Hannah Forsyth, 'continual growth of tertiary education was largely taken for granted as a social and economic good.'[6]

The CRTS educated 300,000 Australians, half of whom attended university. The new Menzies Coalition government continued to press for the expansion of numbers attending higher education, with the goal of shifting the economy away from its dependence on primary industries towards a more generally white-collar workforce. New means-tested Commonwealth scholarships were put in place, intended to make university attendance a reality for talented but poorer students from a much broader range of social and educational backgrounds than previously.[7] Expanding access provided a way to reconcile the demands of the 'rationalists', who wanted to promote economic growth, and the 'populists', who wanted to create opportunities for more Australians.[8] Given the numbers involved, the narrow pathway of matriculation preparation and sitting was overwhelmed; people who would never have dreamed of higher education before were admitted to Australia's universities. The absorption of such numbers was helped by the steady creation of new universities after the war. ANU opened its doors in 1947, soon followed by the University of New South Wales, Monash University and New South Wales University of Technology, while university colleges (attached to the six established universities) were opened in Canberra, Armidale, Newcastle and Wollongong. At the same time, new degrees were created for professions that previously hadn't required university attendance, such as accounting, engineering and pharmacy. Each of these shifts brought university closer to a broader segment of the population, both geographically and in the sense of allowing people to imagine themselves undertaking higher education. The twin processes of easing accessibility while socially mainstreaming the idea of attending university became a default pattern of higher education policy in the decades that followed, to the point where some commentators have argued that Australian society has become 'obsessed' with going to university, expending resources on people who do not need to and will not benefit from attending a higher education institution.[9]

As a more diverse student mix entered university campuses from the 1950s, concerns were raised about whether a greater number from a wider variety of backgrounds would dilute Australian universities' standards. Such concerns recalled similar debates from the late nineteenth century over adding languages other than Latin to the matriculation exam.[10] Traditionalists also lamented the inclusion of 'applied knowledge' disciplines, such as engineering and pharmacy to university curricula. This connection between greater access, broadening curricula, the creation of new universities and diluting standards has been a feature of the debate over universities in Australia ever since.[11] Concerns are regularly raised that the expansion of access to university has flooded Australia's universities with unqualified students, with first-year dropout rates of around one-fifth of enrolled students at some universities cited as evidence that the process of inclusion has gone too far.[12] However, from the beginning of such debates there was little clear evidence that students from more diverse backgrounds were incapable of succeeding at university. Assessments of attrition rates and exam results of CRTS and Commonwealth scholarship students showed that on average they had outperformed students from more privileged backgrounds.[13]

But while expansion of access continued under Labor and Coalition governments, willingness to continue to pay for broadening university education from the public purse evaporated during the 1970s recession. Economist Thomas Piketty observes a similar trend across the developed world, where increasing access to higher education coincided with a freeze on the growth of commensurate public funding. 'As a result,' he argues, 'some who had believed in the promise of expanding access to higher education – often people from modest or middle-class backgrounds – found themselves confronted with dwindling resources and an absence of opportunities after graduation.'[14] For Australians, getting into university might have become easier, but the experience of university was shifting. There would be other, profound consequences for Australia's university sector as well.

Expansion and Stratification

A persistent feature of Australians' university attendance, which sets them apart from culturally similar societies in Europe and North America, is their overwhelming tendency to go to the university that is closest to them geographically. As former University of Melbourne vice-chancellor Glyn Davis observes, Australia has created a tradition of 'commuter universities', attended largely by people who live close by and commute to and from campus.[15] This suggests that there is a cultural proclivity not to discern among universities: if one is happy to attend the most geographically convenient campus, it suggests an attitude that one university is as good as any other. But there are signs that this attitude is starting to be challenged. Regular reports emerge in the national media placing Australia's universities in a hierarchy on a range of measures, from graduate employability to the salary levels of their graduates.[16] One study showed that around four-fifths of Australia's chief executives attended one of its eight 'sandstone' universities.[17] It appears that public awareness of a hierarchy among Australia's universities is emerging, driven by growing attention to university rankings which regularly highlight differences in size, wealth, research performance and entry requirements.[18] Some of the country's universities have started to use certain favourable rankings results in their advertising and recruitment material. At times, public perceptions of some Australian universities are overblown, such as when they are accused of amassing 'Harvard-scale endowments'[19] (Australia's two wealthiest universities have endowments of less than one-tenth of Harvard's US$53.2 billion endowment), but the tendency to compare Australia's university sector with other highly stratified systems has begun. Also notable are occasions in which politicians are compared according to their academic pedigrees:

> Josh Frydenberg's academic achievements with honours in both law and economics (Monash), masters of international relations (Oxford via a Commonwealth scholarship) and masters of public administration (Harvard) far outstrip those of Jim Chalmers, who has a bachelor of arts and a bachelor of communications (Griffith University) and a PhD in political science (Australian National University).[20]

What appears to be happening, under the influence of several factors, is that as the Australian university sector has expanded enrolments and degree possibilities, it has become increasingly vertically differentiated. Foremost is the role of higher education as a 'status good', a class of acquisitions the value of which is created by their scarcity. As economist Fred Hirsch pointed out, expanding access to a status good creates a hierarchy of value: more people may gain access to university places, but then some university places are more prestigious than others.[21] Then there is the influence of the number of professional qualifications being created by universities expanding faster than the employment opportunities beyond the university. As Marginson notes, 'the social opportunities that education is meant to bring are not universal – not in societies that are stratified by unequal earnings and hierarchical power, and where there is an absolute limit to the number of socially advantaged positions on offer.'[22] When there are only so many articled clerkships being offered by the big law firms, competition for places at top law schools intensifies. And third, expansion of the Australian university system coincided with the collapse of governments' willingness to pay for the growth in attendance from public revenues. Older, wealthier universities with long-established catchments of affluent students and benefactors were better placed to prosper in Dawkins' Unified National System than newer, more regional and less well-endowed universities. The advent of the global rankings fifteen years later revealed that certain universities had been in a better position to invest in attributes that would enhance their social and academic esteem: research intensity, facilities, exclusivity, scholarships. The persistent tendency to rank universities and their various components 'entrenches competition for prestige as a principal aspect of the sector and generates circular reputational effects that tend to reproduce the pre-given hierarchy'.[23] Both the Times Higher Education and Quacquarelli Symonds global rankings have installed reputation as a central element in their methodology in their surveys of academics on universities' quality.

Competition for status is integral to academic life, at the university level, the disciplinary level and the individual academic level. The currency of academic access and progression is eminence: the endorsement by academic peers of the value, innovation and quality of one's research. This stands in marked tension with the egalitarian politics of many academics, who advocate for socially progressive causes outside of the university while competing with their colleagues for status and reputation.[24]

The vertical stratification of the Australian university sector is a process that is driven by students and parents as much as by the universities themselves. As universities invest in their own prestige competition, it 'leads to fiercer competition for degrees from those institutions or fields of study which provide better career prospects'.[25] The factors that drive Australian students' choices – such as historical tradition, the preferences of other students, the selectivity of universities' entrance processes – and the reputation of the university among employers, tend to both reinforce and drive the status competition among universities.[26] Prestige also drives stratification among fields of study, with certain degrees, such as medicine and law, commanding much higher entry scores. While government regulation does not permit Australian universities to signal status through price differentials as in the United States, selectivity, as signalled by high entry scores, acts as a powerful proxy. End-of-Year-12 anxieties among students about getting into the 'right' university and degree program continue to rise, with newspapers regularly ranking the 'hardest to get into' degrees across a variety of universities.[27] 'As absolute participation grows,' argues Marginson, 'relative outcome – relative position – kicks in with greater force.'[28] As competition for places intensifies, it favours students from families with more economic, social and cultural advantages. There is a circular economy at play here: 'Leading universities attract leading students and high-achieving staff in an ongoing process of status exchange. The universities draw institutional status from the presence of these valued persons, and apply individual status back to them.'[29] In Australia this has created a clear correlation between the wealth of the university and the wealth of its students' families. Determined to ensure 'intergenerational status maintenance', wealthy families invest in ensuring their children access the most prestigious degree programs at the most prestigious universities.[30] As status competition intensifies, higher education in Australia increasingly plays a social sorting role, reproducing pre-existing social inequalities and legitimating them through appeals to meritocratic achievement. The irony is that expanding access to higher education has magnified stratification:

> In high participation systems two processes of social stratification are brought together. Unequally ranked and valued students are matched with 'appropriate' unequally valued educational opportunity and the unequal social outcomes that follow. An imagined world of free choice and open possibilities is translated into a real world of social allocation and life closure.[31]

The forces driving vertical differentiation and prestige competition among Australia's universities have had the unintended effect of driving all differentiation out of the sector. Despite both Labor[32] and Coalition[33] governments wanting greater diversity in Australia's university sector, the policy frameworks they have designed have worked against this ambition. Creating quasi-markets in prestige goods such as higher education, observes

Marginson, increases vertical differentiation while decreasing horizontal diversity in the sector.[34] As competition favours older, more research-intensive, comprehensive universities, it creates incentives for other universities to emulate that model. Rankings, which confer status on already-prestigious universities, further intensify the pressures on the others to conform to that model in order to compete.[35] This is an irony: greater market competition, according to neoliberal economic theory, should drive diversification; for prestige goods such as higher education, it drives uniformity. It is a perverse outcome of policies that were designed to achieve the opposite effect. Differentiation among universities is a public good, which should allow students from diverse backgrounds and with varied hopes and dreams to find an appropriate niche in higher education, without the pressure of status competition and the invidious comparisons of degrees and institutions. Status competition is stripping this public good out of Australia's higher education sector, replacing it with the increasingly insistent private good of prestige hierarchies.[36]

Battling Privilege

Higher education appears to be where Australian society's two animating ideals, aspiration and egalitarianism, most clearly confront one another. Beginning with the CRTS in the 1940s and continuing through the Whitlam provision of free higher education, these two ideals coincided and reinforced each other, creating a 'universal expectation of personal advance and a better life via learning, a "promethean" culture of [national economic] development and self-development ... in which the limitations of the old self would be transcended and all would be fulfilled'.[37] In conditions of strong economic growth and Keynesian economic management, the belief was widely held that in order to fulfil national development aspirations and widespread desires for personal advancement, people previously not able to attend university should be enabled to do so. Where aspiration and egalitarianism came apart was during the austere 1970s and '80s, when governments' appetites for funding endless expansion of university education dried up. It started to become clear that the abolition of fees by the Whitlam government had not caused a huge rise in under-represented groups at universities as had been expected, and that much of the 'unmet demand' for university places was among less socioeconomically advantaged groups living in outer metropolitan areas of Australia's cities.[38] In tabling his higher education reforms in the 1988 White Paper, *Higher Education: A Policy Statement*, education minister John Dawkins observed that 'inefficiencies arise because significant barriers still exist to the full participation of disadvantaged groups in higher education'.[39]

Coinciding with a major policy statement on social equity and inclusion titled *Towards a Fairer Australia*, achieving greater access to higher education was a significant element in the Dawkins reforms.[40] The White Paper pegged the drive to expand access to university partly to the rationale of bringing greater numbers of people from disadvantaged groups into higher education: 'Improvements in access and equity are heavily dependent on growth in the system. Without new places in the system, it will be difficult to change the balance in the student body to reflect more closely the structure and composition of society as a whole.'[41] The White Paper also acknowledged the need for specific strategies at national, state and institutional levels to ensure some of the extra places were being taken by people from disadvantaged groups. Then in February 1990, Dawkins' department published a companion policy statement titled *A Fair Chance for All: National and Institutional Planning for Equity in Higher Education*.[42] The policy adopted the objective of ensuring that Australians from all groups in society have the opportunity to participate in higher education, and committed the government to 'changing the balance of the student population to reflect more closely the composition of society as a whole'.[43] It specified six disadvantaged groups as the focus for government and university inclusion strategies, setting proportional representation targets for several: people from socio-economically disadvantaged backgrounds; Aboriginal and Torres Strait Islander people; women; people from non-English-speaking backgrounds; people with disabilities; people from rural and isolated areas. The inclusion agenda was justified by reference to both social justice and economic development rationales: 'Australia is moving to strengthen its economic base, with a consequent shift in the traditional profile of our economic activity, so the nation needs a well-educated, skilled and flexible workforce to adjust to these changes. People from disadvantaged groups form a large and diverse pool of under-utilised resources.'[44]

While the government would provide places and financial resources, *A Fair Chance for All* made it clear that it placed a significant part of the responsibility for achieving greater equity in access on the universities themselves. It argued that 'higher education institutions are publicly funded, so they have a clear responsibility to provide opportunities for all sections of the Australian community'. The paper suggested that there needed to be 'behavioural changes on the part of academic and administrative staff,' which needed to 'lead to the acceptance of equity measures as a priority at all levels of planning within the institution'.[45] There was a clear statement that 'achieving a more equitable proportion of disadvantaged people in higher education is consistent with the maintenance of standards', placing the onus on universities to 'ensure that equity measures are targeted at people with the potential to succeed in higher education and provide the learning environment that allows them to graduate'.[46] It required all universities to outline their equity targets and strategies for meeting them as part of their annual agreements with the government.

When the Australian Labor Party returned to government in 2007, the new education minister, Julia Gillard, commissioned a review of Australia's higher education sector. Led by former University of South Australia vice-chancellor Denise Bradley, the review reported that the participation in higher education of people from 'groups disadvantaged by the circumstances of their birth' had been 'static and falling over the last decade'.[47] The figures quoted were stark: in 2007, 1.1 per cent of people from remote areas; 1.3 per cent of Indigenous people; 15 per cent of people of low socioeconomic status; and 18 per cent from rural and regional areas participated in higher education, each of them well below their proportions of the general population. The review noted that these groups were particularly under-represented in the elite Group of Eight universities. With the exception of increasing women's participation, clearly the policies and requirements outlined in *A Fair Chance for All* had not worked. The Bradley review identified a complex mix of situational and attitudinal causes for the lack of progress: 'Barriers to access for [disadvantaged] students include their previous educational attainment, no awareness of the long-term benefits of higher education and, thus, no aspiration to participate.'[48] The report set out clear targets and reporting measures for increasing the access, retention and completion rates of under-represented groups to Australian universities, and called for government and universities to undertake a 'step change' in their approach to facilitating access for these groups by focusing on building awareness of higher education and its benefits, helping to develop wider aspirations to participate and enhancing educational attainment among disadvantaged groups to allow greater participation in higher education.

The government accepted the Bradley review's recommendations, including that universities should be allowed to enrol as many students as they wished, with government funding following where students had been enrolled. The 'demand-driven system' as it became known, resulted in a 70 per cent increase in undergraduate enrolments between 2008 and 2019, but achieved almost no proportional increase in disadvantaged groups. The rate of students with low socioeconomic status backgrounds went from 15.8 per cent to 16.8 per cent; disabled students from 5.4 per cent to 7.7 per cent; Indigenous students from 1.5 per cent to 1.9 per cent; regional students declined from 20.7 per cent to 19.6 per cent; remote students stayed at 0.8 per cent; and students from non-English-speaking backgrounds declined from 3.4 per cent to

3.2 per cent.[49] The familiar patterns of university stratification again reproduced themselves. Despite the increase in undergraduate numbers across the sector during the demand-driven system, domestic enrolments in the elite Group of Eight universities declined, and their proportions of low socioeconomic status students remained lower than the sector average: 8.9 per cent compared with 15.8 per cent in 2008; 9.7 per cent to the sector average of 16.8 per cent in 2019.[50] The data show that lower-ranked universities, particularly in regional areas, are much more likely to admit under-represented groups: 27.1 per cent of students in universities forming the Regional Universities Network came from lower socioeconomic status backgrounds – significantly above the sector average and the quoted rate of pro-rata representation in the population.

Despite decades of government and university efforts to shift them, the patterns of correlation between socioeconomic advantage and university wealth and ranking have stayed stubbornly persistent. A range of reasons have been offered as to why. Simon Marginson suggests the addressing of inequality has been too incremental, fiddling at the edges rather than dealing with a systemic problem: 'The approach is limited to the Pareto optimal, focused on the extension of higher education to social groups that have been under-represented rather than on redistributing access to high-demand higher education institutions.'[51] Or to put it another way, 'for the Australian higher education sector, equity was something to be achieved primarily in the abstract, not in the specific'.[52] There is also the culture of the commuter university: 'Given that Australian tertiary students are relatively immobile and low socioeconomic status students even more so, … fair selection processes do little to counter the socio-geographic reality of a student's environment.'[53] Another challenge is the stratification of educational advantage that occurs at school level in Australia. The pattern of tertiary admissions correlates most strongly with school sector inequalities, with private school graduates gaining a 6 to 8 per cent advantage over government school graduates in their tertiary entrance scores.[54]

The heavy reliance on tertiary entrance scores to select students has also been identified as a barrier to access for under-represented groups. The Bradley review observed, 'the tendency to use the simplest and most defensible approach to admissions (such as [tertiary entrance scores]) has been exacerbated by the high levels of competition for places in some fields of study and the need to be able to defend admissions decisions to external bodies in an increasingly litigious environment.'[55] Numerical tertiary entrance scores are relied on because they provide a transparent, objective and comparable basis for selection, but they also conceal advantage and disadvantage in student circumstances. And as competition intensifies for prestigious degrees and universities, tertiary entrance scores rise to manage demand, thereby privileging the educationally advantaged, with the economic, social and cultural capital to ensure their success at school. Calls are regularly made to scrap or modify the supremacy of numerical scores, but few Australian universities have been willing to innovate radically on their entrance processes.[56] However, perhaps the biggest obstacle to greater inclusion is the logic of higher education as an exclusive good, a logic that is intensified at the elite end of the hierarchy. The stratifying logic is very apparent to disadvantaged groups, which tend to see the sandstone universities as 'being unavailable, an elitist, private school. A lot of kids from disadvantaged backgrounds think that they cannot go to UQ … [they say] "It's not my university. Private school kids go, not me."'[57] For those charged with meeting elite universities' equity targets, the logics are perverse: 'We have set ourselves up as elite and then how do we change that image to being more inclusive and welcoming when we have worked so hard to be elite?'[58]

What those designing higher education policy seem not to have understood is the nature of the university degree as a prestige good, and the corrupting effects of introducing quasi-market competition into the provision of such prestige goods. The effect of expansion and marketisation has been to eliminate variety among types of universities, while increasing the prestige competition, social stratification and returns to economic and social privilege of the higher education sector. These are not results that governments of either side wanted or would want. The social stratification of the Australian tertiary education system cannot be put in the too-hard basket. But actually tackling the issue of inequality of access could be politically perilous: 'No democratic politician commits electoral suicide in frontal conflict with social privilege in education.'[59] The expansion of participation in higher education has widened the economic and social gap between university graduates and non-university graduates.[60] No longer is there an intermediate layer of non-university educated but respected professionals between the tertiary educated and the rest. Further stratification within the Australian university sector, along US lines, could end up having a similar result of widening the education and outcomes gaps among university-educated Australians. There is now a long record of experimentation and failure in ensuring greater access and equity at all levels of the Australian higher education system. This should provide the grist for a new effort and new creativity in changing patterns of social stratification among Australian universities.

The Distance Within

Another form of hierarchy has emerged and become more extreme during the years of the Unified National System, this one within the academic workforce. From its earliest days, the academic workforce in the modern university has been hierarchically organised, with longevity and distinction of service conferring seniority, from professors through readers or associate professors to masters to lecturers. The sociologist Pierre Bourdieu has argued that one of the core tasks of *homo academicus* (as he terms members of the profession) is to control the admission and progress of other academics through the various stages of their careers.[61] What has emerged over the past thirty years, however, is a new form of inequality and precarity within the academic workforce – casualisation. The heavy reliance of Australian universities on a casual academic workforce had been gaining prominence even before the pandemic hit, with analyses suggesting that as much as 63 per cent of the workers at some universities were on either casual or fixed-term contracts.[62] The pandemic brought even greater attention to the precarious plight of casual academic workers, who were the first to lose employment as universities cut spending. More recently, the extensive underpayment of academic casuals has brought intensive attention to the issue of academic casualisation.[63]

While casualisation of the workforce has been a general trend across the economy since the deregulation reforms of the 1980s and '90s, it is clear that the process has been more extensive within universities than in most other public institutions. While university data on the number of casuals employed is opaque, credible analysis argues that around 41 per cent of Australia's academic workforce is on casual or non-continuing contracts.[64] Very high rates of academic casuals surveyed report working unpaid hours, mostly on student consultation, course administration and professional reading and preparation.[65] And while casuals contribute up to half of all teaching at universities, many report not having access to basic teaching resources, such as office space, professional development opportunities and relevant textbooks.[66]

The reasons for the extensive adoption of a casual and non-continuing academic workforce by Australia's universities are many. The pressure to admit ever-increasing numbers of students with declining public funding per student has produced pressures to reduce the cost of teaching.[67] The demand-driven system saw a huge increase in the number of students going to university but no commensurate increase in public funding, while the Job-ready Graduates Package managed to cut the funding for some programs and degrees to below the cost of delivery. Even before the pandemic, universities had to manage the unpredictability of student numbers in courses and programs, with the vagaries of student choices resulting in significant shifts in enrolment and attendance between semesters and years. In this situation, universities have not hired full-time academics to keep pace with rising student numbers, choosing to manage uncertainty and variations with casual and fixed-term staff.[68] Another driver has been research funding, which has become dominated by competitive, fixed-term, project-based grants, particularly in the sciences and engineering. Researchers are hired for the term of the research funding grants, with many spending their careers moving from grant to grant. Some have argued that Australia's universities have built their commanding positions in the global rankings on the backs of an insecure and underpaid research workforce.[69] Within universities, academic work has been fragmented into different components, allowing certain academic tasks to be 'bought out' by those full-time academics who have been successful in securing research funding.[70] What this means is that a casual or fixed-term academic is hired to teach and perform a full-time academic's administrative duties for the duration of the grant. This reflects in turn the devaluation of teaching and the rise in administrative burdens as much as the availability and permissiveness of the 'gig economy' within Australian universities. The oversupply of PhD graduates being produced by those same universities creates a steady supply of willing academic labour.

The casualisation of the academic workforce has been facilitated by the highly decentralised governance of Australia's universities. Decisions on the academic workforce profile are devolved to departments, courses and even individual academics. In political scientist Megan Kimber's memorable phrase, there are decentralised hierarchies consisting of a 'tenured core' and a 'tenuous periphery' now constituting Australia's academic work-force.[71] Tenured academics control the access of casual academics to paid employment, as well as to other resources related to their academic work.[72] The precarity of casual academic work creates an extreme power imbalance between tenured and casual academics, with few oversight mechanisms to ensure this relationship is managed appropriately. The effects on casual academics can be severe. Many work several jobs, supporting dependents, in the hope that their service will eventually result in a rare, tenured academic position. They often struggle to be included in the general academic community, with the conditions and locations of their work often rendering them invisible to the broader discipline. These forms of marginalisation push the dream of academic tenure further and further away.[73]

With several parliamentary inquiries drawing attention to the extent and abuse of academic casualisation at Australian universities, there are clear signs that universities are moving to address this. Several universities have announced the back payment of thousands of hours of unpaid work, and that they will transition casual academics onto more stable and predictable contracts. But this will be an issue that requires ongoing management. Australia's Tertiary Education Quality and Standards Agency (TEQSA) has warned of the risks that 'unusually high reliance on casual staff poses risks for the quality of the student experience'.[74] There are reputational risks also. Commentators have been quick to contrast the high salaries of Australia's vice-chancellors with the low rates of pay and underpayment of casual academics.[75] While certain elements of academic work, such as musical instrument tutors, will continue to rely on casual academics, universities must be vigilant that the driving structural factors for more extensive casualisation remain strong. Ensuring the payment and working conditions of non-tenured academics are appropriate needs to become part of the normal operating systems of Australia's universities. But they have other obligations too. Ensuring that the common marginalisation of non-tenured staff does not occur is as much an obligation of the university as a whole as it is of individual tenured academics. Given current policy and funding frameworks, it is unlikely Australia's higher education sector will move away from employing a significant non-tenured academic workforce; what universities can ensure is that the norms and traditions of academic collegiality and support extend to non-tenured staff.

Universities in Australian Life

In the space of a generation, Australia has been transformed into a majority university-educated society; posing the question of how these high rates of tertiary qualification are changing society. In the course of that thirty years, profound changes have been made to the policy frameworks and funding environments of Australia's universities in order to accommodate this shift, and their effects on the nature of universities and ultimately the relationships of universities to Australian life. University attendance has made Australian society more aspirational but less egalitarian, though shot through with 'a spare sense of entitlement and inclusion and rejection of extremes of either top or bottom'.[76] The expansion of university education in Australia, as in the rest of the Western world, has 'coincided with a reversal of educational cleavage in the voting structure', with the result that tertiary-educated voters are more likely to support parties of the left than the right, while working-class voters have migrated from the left to the right.[77] Thomas Piketty writes of societies like Australia now being dominated by 'duelling elites', a 'Brahmin left' of tertiary-educated progressives, and a 'Merchant right' of highly-paid, wealthy voters, both of which strongly support the society created by deregulation and globalisation over the past three decades: 'both camps are strongly attached to the existing economic system and to globalisation as it is currently organised, which ultimately serves the interests of both intellectual elites and financial elites.'[78] Nick Cater sees a single, tertiary-educated, judgemental elite:

> Having seen off the *bunyip aristocracy*, the Australian social order has been challenged by another prospective patrician class: the *bunyip alumni*, a knowledge-owning nobility that presumes to possess superior insights and manners to the broad mass of people. Its members value brain ahead of brawn, book learning ahead of practical wisdom and look down on those who work with their hands.[79]

Former finance minister Lindsay Tanner believes that widespread university education has divided Australian society between those people who are accustomed to abstract thinking and those who see life in more concrete terms, each of which have had very different experiences of economic reform and globalisation over the past generation.[80]

The growth of university education has coincided with a fundamental shift in Australia's economy and society, which historian and journalist Paul Kelly famously dubbed the 'End of Certainty'.[81] Australia's era of deregulation and economic reform was powered by an intellectual movement that valorised private over public, business over government, and which encompassed both a program of economic and social reform and a piercing critique of the structure and workings of developed societies in the late twentieth century. Under both Labor and Coalition governments, the neoliberal reform movement dismantled the structures of Australia's traditional economy and delegitimised its underpinning ideas and values. In doing so, Australian society was bifurcated into those facing insecure employment and declining wages and working conditions, and an empowered, globally mobile cohort of university-educated professionals.[82] Unsurprisingly, many of the latter cohort became the champions of deregulation and globalisation, as well as its beneficiaries. They also became the main supporters of movements to champion 'sectional equity and emancipation over and above the defence of general living standards and life chances against the floodtide of economic restructuring'.[83] For those supporting the new social justice agendas, the parties of the left offered more sympathetic platforms to advance their political agendas and interests. Here lies the main driver of the reversal of educational levels and voting cleavages observed by Piketty's analysis: 'The most natural explanation is that less educated voters felt that the [left] parties had abandoned them by shifting their attention and priorities to the winners of the educational system and to some extent of globalisation.'[84] But neoliberal

ideas provided a powerful critique of the new left-leaning educated elite also. Public choice theory provided ammunition for
those inclined to be suspicious of publicly educated and publicly
funded elites championing minority interests, directing suspicions
of rent-seeking and hypocrisy towards them. Often these criticisms of left-leaning elites came from right-leaning elites through
the conservative media and talkback radio.[85]

In 1957, Prime Minister Robert Menzies made an appeal to
current and prospective beneficiaries of the expansion of university access: '[University students] will, I am sure, not forget
that … the community is accepting heavy burdens in order that,
through the training of university graduates, the community may
be served.'[86] In the sixty-five years since he made that appeal, the
social licence that he called for – underpinning public support
for expanding Australia's higher education attainment rates – has
eroded. The economic, social and cultural benefits to broader
society of having more of its people tertiary educated have not
been obvious, nor foregrounded in public discussion. University
education is now seen almost universally in terms of individual,
private advantage and achievement, a development reflected in
the slow movement of the funding for universities off the public
balance sheet and onto the students themselves. The counterpart
to this is the evaporation of any sense of responsibility or gratitude among university students and graduates towards the general
public for supporting their education. Expansion of access has created among many students and graduates a sense of entitlement,
that they are owed a university education as a right of their mem-
bership of society. The result is an increasing divide between the

university-educated and the general population that is dangerous for the social licence of Australia's universities and the place they occupy in Australian life.

In the increasingly polarised national conversation we have witnessed over the past decade, clear divisions can be seen between the different camps. As Bri Lee observes, 'the highly educated person's own value system is invisible to them and hyper-visible to those they are speaking down to.'[87] Often tertiary-educated professionals are highly censorious of language or behaviour they regard as unacceptable. As community attitudes on race, gender and sexuality have become more progressive, a new prejudice has arisen against the uncultured and uneducated, a sneering condescension towards anyone regarded as a 'bogan'. As philosopher Michael Sandel observes about the United States,

> Survey research bears out what many working-class voters sensed; at a time when racism and sexism are out of favour (discredited though not eliminated), credentialism is the last acceptable prejudice ... disdain for the poorly educated is more pronounced or at least more readily acknowledged, than prejudice against other disfavoured groups.[88]

While the situation may be less extreme in Australia, it is hard to argue that some version of this is not part of everyday conversations and attitudes across our society. It is a dangerous trend, particularly if it means that widening tertiary education may actually be a divisive force in Australian life. As Barry Hindess and Marian Sawer have observed,

A significant new discourse has emerged in Australian public life, one that focuses on the negative role of elites and the gap between elite values, interests and policy preferences and those of ordinary Australians ... This normalisation of anti-elitist discourse ... represents a profound change in the character of Australian public life.[89]

Australian universities and academics should be aware of this. They and governments must come together to re-create the social licence for widespread tertiary education that Menzies spoke of, or the remit and role of universities in Australian life will soon become even more contested.

Transformation

AT THE END of February 2022, universities across Australia held their first, tentative Orientation Weeks in two years. These were different from the joyous, anarchic 'O-weeks' of February 2020: the 2022 versions were hedged with health restrictions, vaccine mandates, face masks and social distancing; trying to summon a forced spontaneity among students who had been locked down, staring into computer screens for the past two years. The pandemic had been a period of introspection and re-evaluation in Australia as in other societies. The lockdowns had either raised or intensified debates over fundamental social values: gender, race, government–society relations, the authority of scientific expertise, social safety versus individual liberty. And, as we've seen, the role of universities in Australian life. Australia's public conversation crackled with arguments over the purpose and value of higher education; the role of knowledge and expertise in national wellbeing; whether Australia can keep pace with a rapidly changing world; and whether the growing numbers of university-educated Australians are coalescing into a new moralising elite. Beneath these conversations swirled a paradox: as Australia's universities have become more central to contemporary Australia, educating greater numbers than ever before, Australians have become more critical and ambivalent about their universities. The intensity of the dissatisfaction with universities – in newspapers, television, radio, social media and around dinner tables – suggests that for a significant number of Australians, the changes that have occurred to accommodate the expansion of access have dragged universities away from a shared ideal of what they should be. The dissatisfaction with Australia's universities came from the left and the right, from students and employers, from within universities as well as from outside.

Rarely acknowledged or noticed, Australia's universities now occupy an uncomfortably central role in Australian life. They are the focus of individual aspirations and societal ambitions; the sites of acrimonious disputes over what and who we value; pivotal to competing conceptions of what knowledge is for and why it is valuable. Over the past thirty years, as they have moved from the periphery to the centre of Australian life, universities have become subject to a host of competing and contradictory social, policy and academic expectations. They must drive social mobility and inclusion while being committed to individual excellence and meritocratic reward. They should be widely available but socially prestigious. They must deliver high-quality higher education to a large number of Australians but at limited cost to the taxpayer. They need to be institutionally effective and efficient but remain collegial and grounded in non-material academic values. They should be a dynamic export sector that prioritises locals, and the engine of the new economy that still supplies the skills needed by the old.

At the centre of much of the angst about universities lies confrontations between incompatible values: academic versus commercial concerns; collegiality versus competition and corporatisation. Despite consistent attempts by universities to communicate their value to Australian society, and despite public opinion surveys consistently showing public confidence in universities hovering between 70 and 80 per cent for over twenty years, there is clearly a major gulf of trust and understanding between universities and government, and between universities and society.[1] Clearly what universities are communicating about their role, or how they are communicating it, is not resonating, in contrast to many schools, which have built positive and mutually supportive relationships with their local communities over decades.

Destructive Creation?

We stand at the end of a generation of expansion and reform of the Australian university system. The winds of change have been driven by public aspirations and government ambitions, but also by growing confusion about how universities should relate to Australian society more broadly. The journey trodden by each Australian university shows that it 'expands or adjusts itself in response to need, whether the need is sourced in its own internal interest or in the external society'.[2] Over the past thirty years, it has been clear that external imperatives have been much more powerful in shaping universities than internal ones. Government regulation and funding levels and conditions have had a powerful effect: creating, supersizing, corporatising and internationalising universities. Governments of both sides of politics have pressed forward with three broad objectives in higher education policy: to expand the proportion of Australians with tertiary education while maintaining the highest quality of that education; to contain the costs of that expansion to the Australian taxpayer while ensuring universities are kept strictly accountable for that public funding; and to ensure that Australia remains prosperous by reaching the forefront of the fourth industrial revolution. There have been differences between Labor and the Coalition at the margin, with the former pressing harder on social justice and inclusion, and the latter for greater enterprise and choice for universities and students; but both have shared the three core objectives.

To achieve these three broad objectives in higher education, governments of both sides have relied on introducing 'quasi-market' competition into the Australian higher education sector, combined with increasingly demanding and fine-grained regulation. This has been consistent across the Western world, although the anglophone countries have travelled the furthest down the quasi-market route.[3] Beginning with the Dawkins reforms, bounded market principles were seen as the way to square the circle among the disparate expectations government and society had of universities: access, quality and prestige; inclusion and affordability; international influence and national strength; export success while prioritising domestic students. The application of market principles to higher education was based on a range of assumptions. Foremost was that universities are able to deliver economies of scale, providing high-quality education to larger and larger numbers of students by becoming more efficient. Introducing scarcity and competition, along with corporate management, would deliver these efficiencies. Universities, like other utilities, should be able to serve both private and public interests simultaneously; and would soon, it was held, discover that the rewards of commercial success were more effective drivers of innovation than aimless academic inquiry. Many believed that introducing a user-pays element to higher education would increase its value to consumers as well as raising the quality of its provision; and that drawing a clearer link between the specific skills learned and the employment outcomes would increase the individual and aggregate benefits of higher education. It is time to consider whether these assumptions are actually appropriate to higher education.

Many are eager to sheet home the blame for Australia's university paradox to government policy. While this book has documented the Dawkins and post-Dawkins policy frameworks as a major contributor to the current situation, it should not be read as attributing all responsibility to government. Universities have either not resisted or been willing participants in implementing governments' policy frameworks. In the words of one academic reflecting on the post-Dawkins trajectory of universities,

What we must confront in all this is our own responsibility. Are we not the ones who stood by and witnessed the erosion of our hopes and ideals? Did we do anything with determined purpose when we saw our universities being turned into factories in all but name? Did we refuse to fill in the endless questionnaires, to participate in the review committees, to allow ourselves to be measured and quantified, to accept demands that we spell out the path of our future endeavours with ambitious plans to do this and that, to write this, research that, and so on ad infinitum? Did we recoil from competing for the dollars held out to us, to become the servants of industry or whatever other segment of the public weal allegedly demanded what our masters called relevance? Did not some of us rejoice jealously in the alleged excellence of our own institutions while deploring its lack in others? The litany of our supine compliance in the face of manifest tyranny is endless.[4]

But universities' role goes much further than simple acquiescence. They accepted more and more students, focusing on the revenue they brought rather than the effects on education and student engagement. Revenue also made them willing participants in research commercialisation. The corporatisation of the Dawkins reforms saw universities re-create the structures of scarcity and competition within their own organisations, guaranteeing the market logic would reach into all areas of academic life. Locked into competition for status and money, each university viewed and responded to each reform or policy proposal through the lens of how it could benefit or lose, rather than what might be the aggregate effects on higher education in Australia. There is a powerful collective action problem even among just forty-two universities in Australia: with all seeking to maximise their individual benefit, forming a united front has become next to impossible. Reforming education ministers have confronted their staunchest opposition within parliament, not from the university sector.

So what has been the result of the joint embrace of market logics to frame Australia's higher education provision? As we've seen, one clear area where market principles have driven perverse outcomes is in inclusion and equity: higher education as a prestige good has reacted with greater vertical stratification and prestige competition to the expansion of access, in direct contradiction of classic market principles. Another clear result is that there are no economies of scale in higher education. As a labour-intensive service industry, higher education has limited opportunities to benefit from technology-driven efficiencies.[5] Expanding numbers without increasing investment has taken its toll on quality and engagement. And there are other reasons to rethink the bounded market principles that have shaped higher education policy for the last three decades. By commodifying higher education, Australian society is allowing material outcomes to determine what is valuable and what is worthless in our universities. Michael Sandel argues that the application of market principles to institutions or practices where they shouldn't be applied is a form of corruption: 'To corrupt a good or social practice is to degrade it, to treat it according to a lower mode of valuation than is appropriate to it.'[6] He asks, 'What is the moral importance of the attitudes and norms that [markets] may erode or crowd out? Would the loss of non-market norms and expectations change the character of the activity in ways we would (or at least should) regret?'[7] Here it is worth returning to the question posed at the start of the book: in what ways has the expansion of the number of Australians educated at university changed Australian society? On the one hand, the economic benefits have been clear: a larger number of university-educated Australians have made a major contribution to the country's strong economic performance and increasingly complex services sector over the past thirty years. But the political, social and cultural benefits are not so clear. It is difficult, if not impossible, to argue that a more university-educated Australia is more inclusive and egalitarian, culturally sophisticated or public-spirited than it was when university was the preserve of a tiny fraction of Australians.[8] This suggests that university education is no longer creating the public spirit-edness, cultural refinement and open mindedness that were once held to be the great social benefits of higher education. In the spirit of Sandel, we should ask whether we are comfortable with a higher education system that imparts narrow economic value, without delivering broader social, cultural and political benefits to society.

The Wages of Transaction

Some would argue that there's nothing to see here. Does the current state of university–society relations, in which the expanding foot-print of universities in Australian society has created ambivalence and discontent about them, really matter? Are universities simply too sensitive, too craving of affirmation and gratitude?[9] Shouldn't they just shrug at the criticism and ambivalence directed at them by governments and the public? Is there anything wrong with the largely transactional way in which many Australians view their universities? Banks, supermarkets, insurance companies, telecommunications providers, utilities and energy companies aren't well liked by many Australians, but that doesn't stop people using their services and trusting them with their money, financial security and data. Shouldn't universities just relax and adjust to becoming just another service provider among many?

The heat of the debate about universities in recent years suggests the answer to these questions is an emphatic no. While banks, airlines and insurance providers cop regular criticism for what they *do*, universities are subjected to searching and ongoing critique over what they *have become*. There is something about the trend towards the commodification of higher education that does not sit well with many Australians. Universities are not like banks or airlines, which are transactional institutions, easily substituted one for another when the price or the product is favourable. Universities are relational institutions: people aspire to and choose universities to invest a significant portion of the best years of their lives in.[10] Most people only have the chance to study one or perhaps two degrees. The choice they make will be a defining one. People choose a university expecting to develop a relationship that will shape them as a person. I suspect that much of the ambivalence – in both senses of that term – towards universities arises from a sense of disappointment that such a relationship has not developed. Higher education in Australia, for many students, is becoming increasingly transactional – 'How do I get the skills I need to get a high-paying, prestigious job with as little disruption as possible?' – and decreasingly transformational – 'I want to pursue what really interests me and grow personally and intellectually'. While transactional expectations may be more and more prevalent among students, they are increasingly being reinforced by how education is presented by universities. The pressure to specify 'learning outcomes' and to align these with employment outcomes, the endless creation of new degrees ever more narrowly targeted at particular economic niches, the touting of graduate employability rates and mean salary levels, threatens to drag universities in Australia towards being just another service industry.

Without being too dramatic, the trend towards the commodification of higher education spells the end of the university in Australia. If higher education is just a transaction, supplied by just another service industry, there is nothing to stop universities being supplanted by cheaper, more convenient, online purveyors of professional skills. Many have predicted the impending 'disruption' of university business models by online providers for over a decade. The fact that it has not happened, I believe, is because students expect more from a university education: to be part of a cohort of other students who interact inside and outside of the classroom, and to have a transformative university experience. Widespread student dissatisfaction with forced online education during the pandemic has only emphasised the importance of cohorts and life-changing experiences as an expected part of going to university. Universities need to recognise that their survival depends on them delivering what Coursera can never deliver – a maturing educational experience among a selective cohort of fellow students. Universities must stand against the culture of transactionalism in higher education and strive to maintain the transformational, relational aspect of going to university in Australia.

A New Conversation

In August 2021, then Opposition education minister Tanya Plibersek announced that if elected, a future Labor government would seek to establish an Australian Universities Accord to 'end the political bickering over higher education policy',

> The accord would be a partnership between universities and staff, unions and business, students and parents, and, ideally, Labor and Liberal – that lays out what we expect from our universities … The aim of an accord would be to build consensus on key policy questions and national priorities in a sober, evidence-based way, without so much of the political cut and thrust. Building that consensus should help university reform stick.[11]

The proposal of an accord was a deliberate gesture to a landmark achievement by a past Labor government: the negotiation of a Prices and Incomes Accord among the business sector, trade unions and government in 1983 by the Hawke government. It also signalled the intent to embrace the same consensus style of politics that Bob Hawke and his government had pursued. The payoffs for Hawke and his successor Paul Keating were five consecutive election victories and thirteen years in office while overseeing the most sweeping reforms ever made to the Australian economy – reforms that also included the most sweeping reforms ever made to Australia's higher education sector.

The Dawkins reforms occurred in the context of responding to an economic downturn and the need to restructure the Australian economy to adjust to new international economic forces. They were a response to a realisation that Australia's university sector, as it was then constituted, could not deliver what was needed of it. Today, as Australia's economy struggles to remain buoyant amid a global downturn, as global action on climate change raises questions about our dependence on energy and commodities exports, as a fourth industrial revolution driven by innovations largely developed elsewhere portends reshaping society and economy, and as rising geopolitical tensions threaten to disrupt deeply complementary trade patterns, it is time to ask whether Australia's higher education sector is fit for purpose in helping the country navigate its future. Is a sector of forty-two comprehensive, teaching-and-research universities really the most effective way to educate and train large numbers of Australian students to a high standard? The inflationary nature of universities, particularly research-intensive universities, suggests that Australia's university-only model of higher education is a particularly expensive way of providing tertiary education. It is time for Dawkins' creation of a 'unified national system' – converting colleges of advanced education into universities and motivating all universities to conduct research – to be rethought. A more varied higher education ecosystem, such as that in the United States, which has research universities existing alongside technical institutes, liberal arts colleges and community colleges, should be examined as a possible alternative to the unified national system.

There are other questions that need to be asked about the current Australian higher education system. Are universities really the best institutions for achieving equity and social mobility in

Australian society? Is it realistic to expect higher education policy to eliminate status differentiation among inherently elite and prestige-driven institutions? As Simon Marginson argues, in Australia's higher education sector, 'status is the "elephant in the room". No-one can talk about it – even though everyone knows it is there, and that it matters.'[12] Surely providing more and varied opportunities in which students from different backgrounds can find education and training options best suited to their needs and interests is better than pressuring all to find their way through forty-two similar institutions? Are the systems of measurement, regulation and evaluation of university work the right ones to ensure the highest-quality education and engagement of students? The emphasis placed on research goes beyond national policy settings: from formal rankings to evaluation within disciplines and comparative measurement of academic performance, research performance has become the primary indicator of academic performance and prestige. This leads to a concentration at all levels, from whole-of-university down to the individual academic, on maximising research performance, such that all other elements of academic work are regarded as opportunity costs, distracting the institution and the academic from research. When teaching and service are regarded as chores, it is little wonder that student engagement and the cohesion of university communities suffers. While universities and governments can do little to address global pressures to focus on research performance, perhaps there are ways that universities and government can collaborate to redress the balance back to more of an equilibrium between research, teaching and service. These are significant questions, and there are bound to be more. Unless they are addressed with a comprehensive rethink of Australia's higher education sector, the Universities Accord is likely to struggle to achieve more than a temporary reconciliation of the existing contradictory expectations of our universities.

It is necessary for these and other challenges facing Australia's higher education sector to be recognised if we are prepared to have an open public discussion. The obligation on those who are dissatisfied with what universities have become is to be specific about what sort of universities Australia wants and needs. It is apparent that over thirty years of reform there has never been a comprehensive stocktake and discussion about whether the trajectory of Australia's higher education sector is appropriate, desirable and best designed to deliver on the nation's education and research needs. The periodic reviews commissioned by governments of both sides have not been comprehensive investigations of these questions; their terms of reference have stipulated that they should address the workings of the current system in terms of making it more effective, efficient and inclusive. It is unsurprising that the reviews have made recommendations and governments have made policy changes that have left the underlying market-driven framework and contradictory expectations on universities undisturbed.

It will not be easy to begin and sustain such a conversation. The passions surrounding the role and nature of Australia's universities are intense; we can see how quickly discussion can turn into acrimonious criticism and name-calling by looking at the pages of our national newspapers over the past few years. There are many who will be eager to accuse universities of being self-serving and greedy, and others who will rush to impute partisan agendas to governments. It will also be difficult to have a discussion about the intrinsic, non-remunerative elements of universities amid the current obsession with the utilitarian benefits of higher education. Then there is the low political salience of universities in Australia: what politician is going to be prepared to sacrifice time and political capital on rethinking higher education in Australia when the electoral stakes are so low? Consequently, it is the universities that must lead the discussion. They must overcome their collective action problem and adopt the perspective of the higher education sector as a whole, rather than from the interests of their own institutions. This will be the ultimate test of whether they really are Australia's intellectual leaders – the mind of the nation.

ACKNOWLEDGEMENTS

The book you are holding is a piece of self-therapy. I joined the University of Melbourne in November 2019, transitioning from a dean to a deputy vice-chancellor position at the centre of a large university. The change in perspective was profound, requiring me to view the university's operations and fortunes holistically rather than being responsible for one faculty's operations and fortunes.

Then the pandemic hit. I found myself part of an executive team struggling to comprehend the impact of border closures and campus shutdowns on our immediate operations and long-term prospects. Vice-Chancellor Duncan Maskell and Provost Mark Considine asked me to chair a Future State Taskforce to provide the university executive group with advice on the long-term effects of the pandemic on the higher education sector and how the university could best respond to its challenges. In the midst of this, I became aware of the intensification of the anger and criticism being directed towards Australia's universities on traditional and social media. I struggled to comprehend where this anger came from, as institutions so central to society and the economy fought to stay viable.

Along the course of my journey to try to understand why universities seem to occupy such a contested role in Australian life, I was lucky to be able to rely on the generosity of numerous colleagues and friends over many conversations. Fazal Rizvi and I convened a discussion group on the role of universities in society via Zoom in 2020. Participants included Gwilym Croucher, Craig Jeffrey, Jessica Gerrard, Peter McPhee, Siew Fang Law, Simon Marginson, Janet McCalman, Shaun Ewen, Ian Marshman, Nana Oishi and William Locke. It was in the course of these discussions that the idea of writing a book as a way of comprehending what I was experiencing every day came to me.

Further perspectives and ideas were furnished by wide-ranging discussions in the Future State Taskforce, among members that included Pip Nicholson, Shitij Kapur, Mark Considine, Gregor Kennedy, Jim McCluskey, Julie Willis, Nick Blinco, Diana Dalton, Louise Davidson, Jim Watterston and Nilss Olekalns.

A lunch with Chris Feik from Black Inc. – where he delivered his usual flurry of gentle, probing questions – prompted me to write the book proposal. I am grateful to Duncan Maskell for reading the proposal and strongly encouraging me to write the book, and also for numerous conversations with him on many of the themes that run through these pages. Regular dinners with Mark Considine at Jimmy Watson's allowed me to test arguments and collect ideas; Mark was unfailingly generous also in reading and providing incisive comments on all of the draft chapters.

I was lucky to have important conversations with many people with deep understandings of the university sector, higher education policy and Australian society: Subho Banerjee, Gregor Kennedy,

Julie Wells, Glyn Davis, Moira O'Bryan, Andrew Norton, Joanne Wright, Adrian Little, Nicola Phillips, Frank Vetere, Margaret Gardner, David Israel, John Dewar, Tim Lynch, Kate Reynolds. Just as important were friends from outside the sector, who debated with me key arguments of the book: Chris Black, Tony Warren, Sheridan Hume, Nasim Wesley. I also want to thank former government ministers John Dawkins, David Kemp, Brendan Nelson and Lindsay Tanner for giving up their time to be interviewed. I'm especially grateful to Maggie Dawkins for conjuring a delicious lunch on a cold winter's day in Eden Valley to fortify me for the drive back to Adelaide.

Andrew Norton, Robert Manne and Gwilym Croucher read the entire manuscript and provided extensive comments and suggestions. Andrew's comments ran to seventeen close-typed pages and several statistical annexes – surely well beyond the call of duty for a reviewer. Each set of comments greatly strengthened the book. Of course, any remaining inadequacies are entirely my responsibility. Chris Feik, Kate Morgan and the team at Black Inc. have been, as usual, a joy to work with.

I dedicate this book to my sons, Oskar and Felix. Both endured the COVID lockdowns in their final years of schooling and Oskar in his first year of university. Like millions of Australian kids, they have lost irreplaceable years of learning and maturing as part of a cohort of fellow students. That we feel their loss so keenly, and are so determined to restore to them and future generations the educational experience that we had, speaks volumes of the central role of universities in Australian life.

ABOUT THE AUTHOR

As deputy vice-chancellor global, culture and engagement at the University of Melbourne, Professor Michael Wesley provides leadership across the university, with overall responsibility for strategic guidance and expert advice on internationalisation and global engagement.

He is also Professor of Politics. His research and writing focuses on Australian foreign policy and the international affairs of Asia and the Pacific.

Before joining the University of Melbourne, he was dean of the College of Asia and the Pacific at the Australian National University. He has also held positions as the executive director of the Lowy Institute for International Policy, director of the Griffith Asia Institute at Griffith University, and assistant director-general for Transnational Issues at the Office of National Assessments. He has a PhD in international relations from the University of St Andrews.

NOTES

Introduction: Ambivalence

1   Deborah Terry, Address to the National Press Club, Canberra, 26 February 2020.

2   George Megalogenis, *Exit Strategy: Politics after the Pandemic*, Quarterly Essay, Issue 82, 2021, p. 52.

3   Donald Horne, *The Lucky Country*, Sydney: Penguin, pp. 10–11 & 13.

4   Department of Education, Training and Youth Affairs, Higher Education Students Time Series Tables, Canberra, DETYA, 2000.

5   OECD, 'Education at a Glance 2021: OECD Indicators, in Australia', OECD website, https://www.oecd-ilibrary.org/sites/7edf2733-en/index.html?itemId=/content/component/7edf2733-en, accessed 2 February 2023.

6   OECD, Populations with Tertiary Education.

7   Thomas Piketty, *Capital and Ideology*, Cambridge, Massachusetts: Belknap Press, 2020, p. 773 and Amory Gethin, Clara Martinez-Toledano and Thomas Piketty, 'Brahmin Left versus Merchant Right: Changing Electoral Cleavages in 21 Western Democracies, 1948–2020', World Inequality Lab Working Paper No. 2021/15, May 2021.

8   James Button, 'The Educational Divide that Threatens to Split the Left', *The Sydney Morning Herald*, 22 November 2021.

9   Bri Lee, 'Correspondence', Quarterly Essay, Issue 83, 2021, p. 136.

10   Nick Cater, *The Lucky Culture and the Rise of an Australian Ruling Class*, Sydney: HarperCollins, 2013, pp. 25, 27.

11   Sam Roggeveen, *Our Very Own Brexit*, Sydney: Penguin, 2019.

12   Nicholas Biddle and Karuna Reddy, 'Universities in Australia: Attitudes and Challenges', ANU Poll Report No. 29, October 2019, p. 6.

13	Emily Baker, 'Vote Compass Data Shows Climate Change, Cost of Living and the Economy Are the Big Election issues, but Voters Still Split Along Party Lines', ABC News (online), 22 April 2022.

14	Bri Lee, 'Correspondence', p. 136.

15	Interview with John Dawkins, Eden Valley, 3 June 2022; interview with David Kemp, Melbourne, 15 July 2022; interview with Brendan Nelson, Canberra, 18 August 2022; interview with Lindsay Tanner, Melbourne, 14 June 2022.

16	Deloitte Access Economics, *The Importance of Universities to Australia's Prosperity*, October 2015, p. 44.

17	Productivity Commission, *The Demand Driven System: A Mixed Report Card*, Research Paper, June 2019.

18	Andrew Norton, 'What is "Unmet Demand" for University?', 13 July 2007, https://andrewnorton.info/2007/07/13/what-is-unmet-demand-for-university, accessed 2 February 2023.

19	Craig McInnis, Richard James and Robyn Hartley, 'Trends in the First Year Student Experience in Australian Universities', Department of Education, Training and Youth Affairs, 2000, p. 9.

20	Sue Green, 'We Need to Avoid University "Obsession"', *The Age*, 12 June 2020.

21	Chi Baik, Ryan Naylor and Sophie Arkoudis, 'The First Year Experience in Australian Universities: The Experience From Two Decades, 1994–2014', Melbourne Centre for the Study of Higher Education, March 2015, p.2.

22	John Dewar, 'Australia's Universities – Australia's Future', Speech to the National Press Club, Canberra, 6 July 2022.

23	Quoted in Tim Dodd, 'Uni Chief Returns Fire at Coalition's "Foolish" Attacks', *The Australian*, 19 November 2021.

24	Interview with Brendan Nelson, Canberra, 17 August 2022.

25	Sophie Morris, 'Union Targets Marginal Seats', *Australian Financial Review*, 6 September 2004.

26	Jean M. Twenge and Kristin Donnelly, 'Generational Differences in American Students' Reasons for Going to College, 1971–2014: The Rise of Extrinsic Reasons', *Journal of Social Psychology*, 156:6, 2016, pp. 620–29.

27	Andrew Norton, 'Jobs, Interests and Student Course Choices', 21 June 2020, https://andrewnorton.net.au/category/student-interests-preferences/page/2/, accessed 2 February 2023. A preference for double degrees suggests an enduring motivation to combine intellectual interest with employment motives among many young Australians.

28	*The Macquarie Dictionary*, Sydney: Macquarie Library, 1985, p. 96.

29	Sigmund Freud, *Totem and Taboo*, London: Routledge, 2013. My thanks to Mark Considine for bringing Freud's definition of ambivalence to my attention.

30	Geoffrey Blainey, *A Centenary History of the University of Melbourne*, Carlton: Melbourne University Press, 1957; Julie Horne and Geoffrey Sherington, *Sydney: The Making of a Public University*, Carlton: Melbourne University Publishing, 2012.

31	Kate Leihy, *Students, Scholars and Structures: An Early History of the University of Melbourne*, Parkville: University of Melbourne History Department, 2002, p. 8.

32   Émile Durkheim, *Elementary Forms of Religious Life*, Oxford: Oxford University Press, 2008, pp. 38–40

33   '"Brideshead: Top', *The Canberra Times*, 10 June 1982.

34   *The Australian Women's Weekly*, 7 July 1982.

35   Raina Gaind, 'Brideshead First Big Series on Tape', *The Canberra Times*, 3 June 1983.

36   'The Stars Line Up for Brideshead Revisited', *Australian Women's Weekly*, 9 October 1982.

37   Simon Marginson, *Higher Education and the Common Good*, Carlton: Melbourne University Press, 2016, p. 219.

38   Angel Calderon, 'What Will Follow the International Student Boom?', *Australian Universities Review*, 62:1, 2020, p. 21.

39   Department of Education, Skills and Employment figures, 2021. These numbers are equivalent to full-time student load.

40   Chi Baik, Ryan Naylor and Sophie Arkoudis, 'The First-Year Experience in Australian Universities: Findings from Two Decades, 1994–2014', Melbourne Centre for the Study of Higher Education, March 2015, p. 1.

41   Craig McInnes, 'Signs of Disengagement? The Changing Undergraduate Experience in Australian Universities', Inaugural Professorial Lecture, Melbourne Centre for the Study of Higher Education, 13 August 2001.

1: Money

1   Catriona Jackson, 'Don't Nickle and Dime Universities, They are Crucial for Growth', *Australian Financial Review*, 28 August 2018.

2   Interview with David Kemp, Melbourne, 15 July 2022.

3   Robert Griew, 'What Went Wrong? And Where Do We Go Now?' *The Australian*, 11 April 2018.

4   Andrew Norton, 'Recurrent Critiques, Concerns and Crises in Australian Higher Education', 9 December 2020, https://andrewnorton.net.au/?s=waghorne, accessed 2 February 2023, and review of Gwilym Croucher and James Waghorne, *Australian Universities: A History of a Common Cause*, Sydney: UNSW Press, 2020.

5   Interview with John Dawkins, Eden Valley, 3 June 2022.

6   Universities Australia, *2020 Higher Education Facts and Figures*, Canberra: Universities Australia, 2020, p. 25.

7   Monash University, '2021 Annual Report', Council of Monash University, 2021.

8   Department of Education, Skills and Employment, 'Higher Education Trends – Chart Pack', DESE website, accessed 2 February 2023. https://app.powerbi.com/view?r=eyJrIjoiZmY1MjQ3MjktYzUzNC00ZGRlLWJiZDctY2U2NDA2Y-2MzZjZiIiwidCI6ImRkMGNmZDE1LTQ1NTgtNGIxMi04YmFkLWVhMjY5O-DRmYzQxNyJ9.

9   Andrew Norton, 'Why Did Universities Become Reliant on International Students?', 1 June 2020, https://andrewnorton.net.au/2020/06/01/

why-did-universities-become-reliant-on-international-students-part-1-government-funding-cuts/, accessed 2 February 2023.

10   Glyn Davis, *The Australian Idea of a University*, Melbourne: Melbourne University Press, 2017.

11   Davis, *The Australian Idea of a University*, p. 79.

12   Sheila Slaughter and Larry L. Leslie, *Academic Capitalism: Politics, Policies and the Entrepreneurial University*, Baltimore: The Johns Hopkins University Press, 1997, p. 17.

13   Ben Wildavsky, *The Great Brain Race: How Global Universities are Reshaping the World*, Princeton: Princeton University Press, 2010, pp. 23–36.

14   Simon Marginson, 'Equity, Status and Freedom: A Note on Higher Education', Cambridge: *Cambridge Journal of Education*, 41:1, 2011, p. 31.

15   Frans van Vught, 'Mission Diversity and Reputation in Higher Education', *Higher Education Policy*, 21:2, 2008, p. 169.

16   Marginson, *Higher Education and the Common Good*, p. 222.

17   Slaughter and Leslie, *Academic Capitalism*, p. 9.

18   Robert Griew, 'Uniformity in Regulations Diminishes Academic Diversity', *The Australian*, 24 October 2018.

19   Norton, 'Recurrent Critiques, Concerns and Crises in Australian Higher Education'.

20   Howard R. Bowen, *The Costs of Higher Education: How Much do Universities Spend per Student and How Much Should They Spend?*, Washington: Jossey-Bass Publishers, 1980, pp. 19–20.

21   Simon Marginson, *Educating Australia: Government, Economy and Citizen since 1960*, Cambridge: Cambridge University Press, 1997, p. 28.

22   Marginson, *Educating Australia*, p. 30

23   Marginson, *Educating Australia*, p. 44

24   Commonwealth Tertiary Education Commission, *Recommendations for the 1984 Supplementary Report on Participation Initiatives in Higher Education*, Belconnen: CTEC, 1983.

25   Interview with John Dawkins, Eden Valley, 3 June 2022.

26   Bob Hawke, 'Policy Speech: Federal Election Campaign Launch', Sydney Opera House Theatre, 16 February 1983, p. 20, National Library of Australia NL pbk c.1.

27   Stuart MacIntyre, André Brett and Gwilym Croucher, *No End of a Lesson: Australia's Unified National System of Higher Education*, Carlton: Melbourne University Publishing, 2017, pp. 3–4.

28   Interview with John Dawkins, Eden Valley, 3 June 2022.

29   MacIntyre, Brett and Croucher, *No End of a Lesson*, p. 4.

30   Margaret Gardner, 'International' in Gwilym Croucher, Simon Marginson, Andrew Norton and Julie Wells (eds), *The Dawkins Revolution 25 Years On*, Carlton: Melbourne University Press, 2013, pp. 268–69.

31   Interview with John Dawkins, Eden Valley, 3 June 2022.

32	R. Jackson, *Report of the Committee to Review the Australian Overseas Aid Program*, Canberra: AGPS, 1984, p. 11.

33	Gardner, 'International', p. 269.

34	Interview with John Dawkins, Eden Valley, 3 June 2022.

35	John Dawkins, *Higher Education: A Policy Statement*, Canberra: AGPS, 1987, p. 75.

36	Dawkins, *Higher Education*, p.75.

37	Interview with John Dawkins, Eden Valley, 3 June 2022.

38	Neville Wran, *Report of the Committee on Higher Education Funding*, Canberra: AGPS, 27 April 1988.

39	Ross Williams, 'System Funding and Institutional Allocations', in Gwilym Croucher, Simon Marginson, Andrew Norton and Julie Wells (eds), *The Dawkins Revolution 25 Years On*, p. 95.

40	Bruce Chapman and Jane Nichols, 'HECS' in Croucher, Marginson, Norton and Wells (eds), *The Dawkins Revolution 25 Years On*.

41	Leslie Harold Martin et al., *Tertiary Education in Australia: Report of the Committee on the Future of Tertiary Education in Australia*, Melbourne: Australian Universities Commission, 27 August 1964.

42	Susan Davies, *The Martin Committee and the Binary Policy of Higher Education in Australia*, Melbourne: Ashwood House, 1989, p. 147.

43	Gwilym Croucher and James Waghorne, *Australian Universities: A History of a Common Cause*, Sydney: UNSW Press, 2020, p. 126.

44	Norton, 'Why Did Universities Become Reliant on International Students?'.

45	Quoted in MacIntyre, Brett and Croucher, *No End of a Lesson*, p. 154.

46	Of course both Britain and the US established state universities through the nineteenth and twentieth centuries, but their first universities were private, ecclesiastical institutions.

47	Quoted in Hannah Forsyth, *A History of the Modern Australian University*, Sydney: NewSouth Books, 2014, p. 10.

48	Croucher and Waghorne, *Australian Universities*, p. 10.

49	Forsyth, *A History of the Modern Australian University*, p. 53.

50	Keith A.H. Murray, Ian Clunies-Ross, Charles R. Morris, Alex I Reid and J. C. Richard, *Report of the Committee on Australian Universities*, Melbourne: Committee on Australian Universities, 1957.

51	Robert Menzies, 'Australian Universities: Ministerial Statement in Connection with the Report of Committee', 28 November 1957, Canberra: Commonwealth Government Printer, 1957.

52	Menzies, 'Australian Universities'.

53	Marginson, *Educating Australia*, p. 42

54	Piketty, *Capital and Ideology*, p. 241.

55	Simon Marginson, 'The Limitations of Human Capital Theory', *Studies in Higher Education*, 44:2, 2019, p. 292.

56	Milton Friedman, *Capitalism and Freedom*, Chicago: University of Chicago Press, 1962.

57   Malcolm Fraser and Margaret Simons, *Malcolm Fraser: The Political Memoirs*, Melbourne: Melbourne University Press, 2015, p. 241. My thanks to Andrew Norton for drawing my attention to this quote.

58   Roderick West, Gary Banks, Peter Baume, Lachlan Chipman, Clem Doherty and Kwong Lee Dow, *Learning for Life: Review of Higher Education Financing and Policy, Final Report*, Canberra: Department of Employment, Education, Training and Youth Affairs, 1998, pp. 77–98.

59   *Fightback! Supplementary Papers*, Canberra: Liberal Party of Australia, 1991, pp. 44–45.

60   David Kemp, Proposals for Reform in Higher Education, Appendix 4, Leaked Cabinet Submission, October 1999.

61   Denise Bradley, Peter Noonan, Helen Nugent and Bill Scales, *Review of Australian Higher Education Final Report*, Canberra: Department of Education, Employment and Workplace Relations, 2008.

62   David Kemp and Andrew Norton, *Review of the Demand-driven Funding System*, Final Report, Canberra, 2013.

63   Andrew Norton, 'After Demand-driven Funding in Australia', HEPI Report 128, 10 May 2020.

64   Interview with David Kemp, Melbourne, 15 July 2022.

65   Interview with Lindsay Tanner, Melbourne, 14 June 2022.

66   Tim Dodd, 'International Students' Cash Can't Last, Universities Told', *The Australian*, 28 August 2018.

67   John Roskam, 'No Need to Bail Out Bloated Unis', *Australian Financial Review*, 6 March 2020.

68   Robert Bolton, 'Uni Vice-Chancellor Salaries "Ridiculous"', *Australian Financial Review*, 16 November 2020.

69   Piketty, *Capital and Ideology*, p. 543.

70   My thanks to Andrew Norton for this point.

2: Value

1   Larry Siedentop, *Inventing the Individual: The Origins of Western Liberalism*, London: Penguin Books, 2015, p. 234.

2   Forsyth, *A History of the Modern Australian University*, p. 125.

3   Simon Marginson and Mark Considine, *The Enterprise University: Power, Governance and Reinvention in Australia*, Cambridge: Cambridge University Press, 2000.

4   Gwilym Croucher and James Waghorne, *Australian Universities: A History of a Common Cause*, Sydney: UNSW Press, pp. 29–30.

5   Menzies, 'Australian Universities: Ministerial Statement in Connection with the Report of Committee'.

6   Steven Brint, *In an Age of Experts: The Changing Role of Professionals in Politics and Public Life*, Princeton: Princeton University Press, 1994, p. 7

7   Richard Hofstadter, *Academic Freedom in the Age of the College*, New Brunswick: Transaction Publishers, 1996.

8   Brint, *In an Age of Experts,* p. 6.

9   Croucher and Waghorne, *Australian Universities,* p. 41.

10   Conrad Russell, *Academic Freedom*, London: Routledge, 1993, p. 8.

11   Richard Hofstadter, *Anti-Intellectualism in American Life*, New York: Vintage Books, 1962, p. 7.

12   Hofstadter, *Anti-Intellectualism in American Life,* p. 25.

13   Marginson and Considine, *The Enterprise University,* p. 54.

14   Stefan Collini, *What Are Universities For?*, London: Penguin, 2012, p. 198.

15   MacIntyre, Brett and Croucher, *No End of a Lesson,* p. 39.

16   MacIntyre, Brett and Croucher, *No End of a Lesson*, p. 41.

17   Quoted in Paul Kelly, *The End of Certainty*, Sydney: Allen & Unwin, 1994, p. 196.

18   Quoted in MacIntyre, Brett and Croucher, *No End of a Lesson,* p. 32.

19   World Bank, *The East Asian Miracle: Economic Growth and Public Policy*, Oxford: Oxford University Press, 1993.

20   John Dawkins, 'Higher Education in Australia: Ministerial Statement', *Hansard*, 22 September 1987.

21   J.S Dawkins, *Higher Education: A Policy Discussion Paper*, Canberra: Australian Government Publishing Service, 1987, p. iii.

22   Interview with John Dawkins, Eden Valley, 3 June 2022.

23   Dawkins, *Higher Education: A Policy Discussion Paper*, p. 1.

24   MacIntyre, Brett and Croucher, *No End of a Lesson,* p.18

25   Marginson and Considine, *The Enterprise University,* p. 54.

26   Dawkins, *Higher Education: A Policy Discussion Paper*, p. 47.

27   Marginson and Considine, *The Enterprise University,* p. 61.

28   Dawkins, *Higher Education: A Policy Discussion Paper*, p. 50.

29   Dawkins, *Higher Education, A Policy Discussion Paper,* p. 51.

30   Les Bell and Howard Stevenson, *Education Policy: Process, Themes and Impact*, London: Routledge, 2006, pp. 76–77.

31   J.S. Dawkins, *Higher Education: A Policy Statement*, Canberra: Australian Government Publishing Service, 1988, p. 101.

32   Dawkins, *Higher Education: A Policy Statement*, p. 104.

33   MacIntyre, Brett and Croucher, *No End of a Lesson*, p. 108.

34   Dawkins, *Higher Education: A Policy Statement*, p. 101.

35   Dawkins, *Higher Education: A Policy Statement*, p. 102.

36   Interview with John Dawkins, Eden Valley, 3 June 2022.

37   Dawkins, *Higher Education: A Policy Statement*, p. 103.

38   Marginson and Considine, *The Enterprise University*, pp. 35–36.

39   Interview with John Dawkins, Eden Valley, 3 June 2022.

40   Marginson and Considine, *The Enterprise University*, p. 21.

41   Marginson and Considine, *The Enterprise University*, p. 35.

42   Interview with John Dawkins, Eden Valley, 3 June 2022.

43 PhillipsKPA, *Review of Reporting Requirements for Universities, Final Report*, Richmond: PhillipsKPA Pty Ltd, December 2012.

44 Forsyth, *A History of the Modern Australian University*, p. 148.

45 Slaughter and Leslie, *Academic Capitalism*, 1997.

46 Marginson and Considine, *The Enterprise University*, p. 36.

47 My thanks to Mark Considine for this point.

48 Marginson and Considine, *The Enterprise University*, p. 20

3: Loyalty

1 Hazel Ferguson and Harriet Spinks, 'Overseas Students in Australian Higher Education: A Quick Guide', Australian Parliamentary Library, 22 April 2021, https://www.aph.gov.au/About_Parliament/Parliamentary_ Departments/Parliamentary_Library/pubs/rp/rp2021/Quick_Guides/ OverseasStudents#:~:text=This%20quick%20guide%20provides%20an,over- seas%20student%20enrolments%20in%202020, accessed 2 February 2023.

2 Robert Bolton, 'Pushback Against International Students', *Australian Financial Review*, 25 February 2019.

3 Tim Pitman, '"Profitable for the Country": An Australian Historical Perspective of the Contested Purpose of Public Universities', *Higher Education Research and Development*, 39:1, 2020, pp. 13–25.

4 Croucher and Waghorne, *Australian Universities*, pp. 12–13.

5 Julia Horne, 'How Universities Came to Rely on International Students', *The Conversation*, 22 May 2020.

6 Lyndon Megarrity, 'Regional Goodwill, Sensibly Priced: Commonwealth Policies Towards Colombo Plan Scholars and Private Overseas Students, 1945–72', *Australian Historical Studies*, 38:129, 2007, p. 97

7 Megarrity, 'Regional Goodwill, Sensibly Priced'.

8 See for example Gwenda Tavan, 'Immigration: Control or Colour Bar? The Immigration Reform Movement, 1959–1966', *Australian Historical Studies*, 32:117, 2001, pp. 181–200.

9 Australian Government, *National Strategy for International Education*, Canberra, 2016.

10 Marginson, *Educating Australia*, p. 238.

11 Ian Marshman and Frank Larkins, 'Modelling Individual Australian Universities Resilience in Managing Overseas Student Revenue Losses from the COVID-19 Pandemic', Centre for the Study of Higher Education, University of Melbourne, 2020, https://melbourne-cshe.unimelb.edu. au/__data/assets/pdf_file/0009/3392469/Australian-Universities-COVID-19- Financial-Management.pdf, accessed 2 February 2023.

12 Andrew Norton, 'How Reliant is Australian University Research on International Student Profits?', 21 May 2020, https://andrewnorton.net. au/2020/05/21/how-reliant-is-australian-university-research-on-international- student-profits/, accessed 2 February 2023.

13   Tim Dodd, 'Australia's "Big Five" Universities are Pulling Away from the Rest', *The Australian*, 17 August 2022.

14   Anthony Welch, 'A Plague on Higher Education? COVID, Camus and Culture Wars in Australian Universities', *Higher Education Quarterly*, 76, 2022, p. 222.

15   Anthea Roberts, *Is International Law International?*, Oxford: Oxford University Press, 2017, pp. 52–72.

16   Lei Hou, Yueling Pan and Jonathan J.H. Zhu, 'Impact of Scientific, Economic, Geopolitical and Cultural Factors on International Research Collaboration', *Journal of Infometrics*, 15, 2021, p. 2.

17   Leonardo Costa Ribiero, Márcia Siqueira Rapini, Leandro Alves Silva and Eduardo Motta Albuquerque, 'Growth Patterns of the Network of International Collaboration in Science', *Scientometrics*, 144:1, 2018, pp. 159–79.

18   Caroline S. Wagner, Travis A. Whetsell and Satyam Mukherjee, 'International Research Collaboration: Novelty, Conventionality and Atypicality in Knowledge Recombination', *Research Policy*, 48, 2019, p. 1261.

19   Kaihua Chen, Yi Zhang and Xiaolan Fu, 'International Research Collaboration: An Emerging Domain of Innovation Studies?', *Research Policy*, 48, 2019, p.158.

20   Marek Kwiek, 'Internationalists and Locals: International Research Collaboration in a Resource-Poor System', *Scientomentrics*, 124, 2020, p. 59.

21   A. Gorska, P. Korzynski, G. Mazurek and F. Pucciarelli, 'The Role of Social Media in Scholarly Collaboration: An Enabler of International Research Team's Activation?', *Journal of Global Information Technology Management*, 23:4, 2020, p. 5.

22   James Laurenceson and Michael Zhou, 'The Australia-China science boom', Australia-China Relations Institute, University of Technology, Sydney, July 2020.

23   Wagner, Whetsell and Mukherjee, 'International Research Collaboration', p. 1261.

24   Chen, Zhang and Fu, 'International Research Collaboration', p. 154.

25   Duanhong Zhang, Wenjia Ding, Yang Wang and Siwen Lu, 'Exploring the Role of International Research Collaboration in Building China's World-Class Universities', *Sustainability*, 14: 3487, March 2022, p. 13

26   Zhang, Ding, Wang and Lu, 'Exploring the Role of International Research Collaboration in Building China's World-Class Universities', p. 10.

27   Megarrity, 'Regional Goodwill, Sensibly Priced', p. 98.

28   Tim Dodd, 'Unis Face an Invidious Choice', *The Australian*, 21 February 2018.

29   Welch, 'A Plague on Higher Education?', p. 216.

30   Megarrity, 'Regional Goodwill, Sensibly Priced', p. 103.

31   Interview with John Dawkins, Eden Valley, 3 June 2022.

32   *The Age*, Letters, 12 May 2021.

33   Megarrity, 'Regional Goodwill, Sensibly Priced', p. 101.

34   For example, *The Australian*, Letters, 14 January 2020.

35   Alan Tudge, 'Challenges and Opportunities in International Education', Speech delivered at RMIT, Melbourne, 31 March 2021.

36 *The Australian*, Letters, 29 April 2020.

37 *The Australian*, Letters, 12 April 2021.

38 For example, Judith Sloan, 'Pandemic Proves "Big Australia" is a Mistake', *The Australian*, 11 May 2021.

39 Abul Rizvi, 'The Dirty Jobs below Our Dignity', *The Sydney Morning Herald*, 18 June 2021.

40 *The Australian*, Letters, 3 August 2020.

41 For example Judith Sloan, 'Turnbull's Failure Was Not to Put Australian Interests First', *The Australian*, 24 August 2018.

42 Agnes Bodis, 'The Discursive (Mis)representation of English Language Proficiency', *Australian Review of Applied Linguistics*, 44:1, 2021, p. 45.

43 Michael Haugh, 'Complaints and Troubles Talk about the English Language Skills of International Students in Australian Universities', *Higher Education Research and Development*, 35:4, 2016, p. 728.

44 John Ross, '"Time to Go Home", Australian PM Tells Foreign Students', Timeshighereducation.com, 3 April 2020.

45 For example, Peter Hurley, 'In Tertiary Education, Investment Reaps Rewards', *The Age*, 5 April 2021.

46 Bodis, 'The Discursive (Mis)representation of English Language Proficiency', pp. 38–39.

47 Brigid Freeman, Ian Teo and Dong Kwang Kim, 'A Review of Australia's Response to International Student Needs During the COVID19 Pandemic in 2020', *Australian Universities' Review*, 64:1, 2021.

48 Marginson, *Educating Australia*, p. 234

49 Mark Mallman, Andrew Harvey, Giovanna Szalkowicz and Anthony Moran, 'Campus Convivialities: Everyday Cross-cultural Interactions and Symbolic Boundaries of Belonging in Higher Education', *Studies in Higher Education*, 2019.

50 Ghazalossadat Fatemi and Eisuke Saito, 'Unintentional Plagiarism and Academic Integrity: The Challenges and Needs of Postgraduate International Students in Australia', *Journal of Further and Higher Education*, 44:10, 2020, pp. 1305–19.

51 Alex Joske, 'Picking Flowers, Making Honey' Australian Strategic Policy Institute, October 2018, https://www.aspi.org.au/report/picking-flowers-making-honey, accessed 2 February 2023.

52 'China's Campus Mischief is a Security Wake-up Call', *The Australian*, 25 August 2020.

53 *The Australian*, Letters, 25 August 2020.

54 Andrew Clark, 'China Doves and Hawks Go to War', *Australian Financial Review*, 5 May 2018.

55 Peter Jennings, 'Control over China Policy Threatened', *The Australian*, 3 November 2018.

56 'It's a Relief This Foreign Interference Thing Isn't Heavy-handed or Sinophobic', *The Australian*, 15 November 2019.

57 Paul Monk, 'The West, a Primer', *The Australian*, 28 July 2018.

58 Jim Molan, 'Greens Want to Surrender Our National Security with the Dumbest of Policies', *The Australian*, 5 April 2019.

59 Phillip Coorey, 'Uni Crisis Talks as China Espionage Fears Grow', *Australian Financial Review*, 21 August 2019.

60 *The Australian*, Letters, 2 June 2020.

61 Max Maddison and Steve Jackson, 'Foreign Students Bullying Lecturers', *The Australian*, 5 August 2020.

62 Joseph Brookes, 'Minister Rejects Six Peer-reviewed ARC Research Grants on "National Interest" Grounds', InnovationAus.com, 24 December 2021.

63 Angel Calderon, 'What Will Follow the International Student Boom?', *Australian Universities Review*, 62:1, 2020, pp. 23–24.

4: Integrity

1 See Hannah Forsyth, 'The Russel Ward Case: Academic Freedom in Australia During the Cold War', *History Australia*, 11:3, 2014, pp. 31–52.

2 Darren L. Linville and Will J. Grant, 'The Role of Student Academic Beliefs in Perceptions of Instructor Ideological Bias', *Teaching in Higher Education*, 22:3, 2017, p. 3.

3 Jennifer Oriel, 'Muting Free Speech a Dark Cloud over the West', *The Australian*, 30 November 2020.

4 *The Australian*, Letters, 8 June 2018.

5 Bella D'Abrera quoted in Rebecca Urban, 'Ideology Strangles Courses at Unis', *The Australian*, 16 January 2021.

6 *The Australian*, Letters, 4 January 2018; 20 August 2018; 6 April 2019.

7 Tom Switzer, Charles Jacobs, 'It is Wilful Ignorance – How Universities are Betraying Australia', *The Australian*, 21 June 2018.

8 Paul Kelly, 'Lessons in Failure', *The Australian*, 24 July 2021.

9 Nick Cater, *The Lucky Culture*; Bri Lee, 'Correspondence'.

10 Matthew Lesch, 'Uni Regulator's Been Hijacked' *The Australian*, 29 June 2018; Urban, 'Ideology Strangles Courses at Unis'.

11 Adam Creighton, 'How the West Became More Like China', *The Australian*, 2 March 2021.

12 Morgan Begg, 'Ridd's Fight Against Groupthink is One for History Books', *The Australian*, 25 June 2021.

13 *The Australian*, 20 September 2019.

14 Nick Cater, 'By Muzzling Dissent, Tech Giants Only Feed Fears of Conspiracy', *The Australian*, 19 October 2021.

15 Aaron Patrick, 'Economists Fight over Life, Death and their Reputations', *Australian Financial Review*, 28 May 2020.

16 Skye Laris, quoted in Phillip Coorey, 'Thrills and Spills', *Australian Financial Review*, 5 October 2018.

17 Quoted in Jill Rowbotham, 'Unis Warned Government Biggest Threat to "Freedom"', *The Australian*, 12 February 2020.

18   Linville and Grant, 'The Role of Student Academic Beliefs in Perceptions of Instructor Ideological Bias', p. 3.

19   Margaret Sheil, 'Academic Independence Even More Precious in the Era of Fake News', *The Australian*, 6 June 2018.

20   *The Australian*, Letters, 22 June 2018.

21   Peter van Onselen, 'Denying Unis a Lifeline is Ideological Wilful Ignorance', *The Australian*, 25 April 2020.

22   *The Age*, Letters, 15 October 2021.

23   Jacqueline Maley, 'All a Game for the Culture Warriors', *The Age*, 30 June 2018.

24   Tim Dodd, 'Odd How These Post-truth Institutions Turned Out to Be Right All Along', *The Australian*, 24 February 2021.

25   'Let's Tear it All Down at the Dawn of Great Awakening', *The Australian*, 13 June 2020.

26   Brendan O'Neill, 'Woke Mobs Rise up in War on the West', *The Australian*, 13 June 2020.

27   Rosemary Sage, 'A New Woke Religion: Are Universities to Blame?', *Journal of Higher Education Policy and Leadership Studies*, 3:2, 2022, p. 31.

28   My thanks to Robert Manne for this point.

29   Michael A. Peters, 'Leo Strauss and the Neoconservative Critique of the Liberal University: Postmodernism, Relativism and the Culture Wars', *Critical Studies in Education*, 49:1, March 2008, p. 14.

30   Allan Bloom, *The Closing of the American Mind: How Higher Education Has Failed Democracy and Impoverished the Souls of Today's Students*, New York: Simon and Schuster, 1987.

31   Urban, 'Ideology Strangles Courses at Unis'.

32   Janet Albrechtsen, 'University Fail', *The Australian*, 31 August 2019.

33   Tom Switzer, 'Cancel Culture is Destroying Our Society', *The Australian*, 16 April 2021.

34   Samantha Hutchinson, 'Victory for Free Speech as Uni Lifts Ban on Talk Rejecting Rape Crisis', *The Australian*, 2 August 2018.

35   Joe Kelly and Richard Ferguson, 'A Black and White Case of "Identity Politics"', *The Australian*, 13 June 2018.

36   Greg Brown, 'Universities in Long March to the Left, Josh Frydenberg says', *The Australian*, 17 June 2018.

37   Tanveer Ahmed, 'Big Government Conservatism', *Australian Financial Review*, 6 December 2021.

38   Verity Burgmann, *Power and Protest: Movements for Change in Australian Society*, Sydney: Allen & Unwin, 1993, p. 4.

39   Burgmann, *Power and Protest*, pp. 6–7.

40   Burgmann, *Power and Protest*, p. 7.

41   Hannah Forsyth, *A History of the Modern Australian University*, p. 77.

42   Clark Kerr, *The Uses of the University*, p. 217.

43 John R. Searle, 'Rationality and Realism: What is at Stake?', *Daedalus*, 122:4, Fall 1993, p. 71.

44 For example Rebecca Urban, 'Fine Unis for Caving on Free Speech', *The Australian*, 18 June 2021.

45 See Bri Lee, *Who Gets to Be Smart?* Sydney: Allen & Unwin, 2021.

46 Anthony Galloway, 'Uni Paper Caught in Row over Chinese Links Report', *The Age*, 6 April 2021.

47 Stephen Chavura, 'We Must Gather the Courage to Confront "Cancel Culture" Mob', *The Australian*, 9 April 2021.

48 'University Lesson in Free Speech', *The Australian*, 30 July 2021.

49 Aaron Patrick, 'China Activist Loses Appeal Against UQ Suspension', *The Australian*, 15 July 2020.

50 Gideon Rozner, 'Ridd Challenge Goes to the Heart of a Free Society', *The Australian*, 29 July 2020.

51 *The Age*, Letters, 19 October 2019.

52 Jacqui Hoepner, 'Silencing Behaviours in Contested Research and Their Implications for Academic Freedom', *Australian Universities Review*, 61:1, 2019.

53 Andrew Miller, 'Academic Freedom: Defending Democracy in the Corporate University', *Social Alternatives*, 38:3, 2019, p. 3.

54 Rob Watts, 'What Crisis of Academic Freedom? Australian Universities After French', *Australian Universities' Review*, 63:1, 2021, p. 11.

55 Hilde de Ridder Simoens (ed.), *A History of the University in Europe: Volume 1 Universities in the Middle Ages*, Cambridge: Cambridge University Press, 1992.

56 Adrienne Stone, 'Before the High Court: The Meaning of Academic Freedom: The Significance of *Ridd v James Cook University*', *Sydney Law Review*, 43:2, 2021, pp. 252–53.

57 Australian Government, *Higher Education Support Act*, 2003, No. 149, 2003, https://www.legislation.gov.au/Details/C2022C00005.

58 See *The Australian*, Letters, 10 January 2020.

59 Stone, 'Before the High Court', p. 254.

60 Conrad Russell, *Academic Freedom*, p. 16.

61 Fred D'Agostino and Peter Greste, 'Slippery Beasts: Why Academic Freedom and Media Freedom Are So Difficult to Protect', *Australian Universities' Review*, 63:1, 2021, p. 46. Italics in the original.

62 D'Agostino and Greste, 'Slippery Beasts', p. 47. Italics in the original.

63 'ANU Responds to Criticism Over Centre for Western Civilisation Decision', *7:30 Report*, ABC TV, 7 June 2018, https://www.abc.net.au/7.30/anu-responds-to-criticism-over-centre-for-western/9847018.

64 Tony Abbott, 'Paul Ramsay's Vision for Australia', *Quadrant*, 24 May 2018, p. 2.

65 Abbott, 'Paul Ramsay's Vision for Australia', p. 4. Italics in the original.

66 'The ANU Must Enlighten Us on a Strange Decision', *Australian Financial Review*, 9 June 2018.

NOTES

67 Greg Sheridan, 'This is an Infamous, Dishonest and Wholly Untrue Charge',
The Australian, 8 June 2018.

68 Kevin Donnelly, 'The West is Lost and Our Unis Founder in Farce',
The Australian, 12 June 2018.

69 *The Australian*, Letters, 29 July 2019.

70 Nick Cater, 'Australian Success Story Offers No Scope for Contrition or Cringe',
The Australian, 23 January 2018.

71 Gareth Evans and Brian Schmidt, 'Why ANU Knocked Back the Ramsay Centre
Proposal', *The Australian*, 26 June 2018.

72 Evans and Schmidt, 'Why ANU Knocked Back the Ramsay Centre Proposal'.

73 Newman, *The Idea of a University*.

74 Andrew G. Bonnell, 'The Ramsay Centre and "Western Civilisation"', *Australian
Universities' Review*, 61:2, 2019, pp. 66–67.

75 Jamie Cohen-Cole, *The Open Mind: Cold War Politics and the Sciences of Human
Nature*, Chicago: University of Chicago Press, 2014.

76 Bonnell, 'The Ramsay Centre and "Western Civilisation"', p. 67.

77 Abbott, 'Paul Ramsay's Vision for Australia', p. 4.

78 Ivan Head, 'The Ramsay Centre and Open Inquiry', *Quadrant*, 22 October 2018,
p. 3

79 Henry Maher, Eda Gunyadin and Jordan McSwiney, 'Western Civilisationism
and White Supremacy: The Ramsay Centre for Western Civilisation', *Patterns of
Prejudice*, 55:4, 2021, p. 316.

80 Evans and Schmidt, 'Why ANU Knocked Back the Ramsay Centre Proposal'.

81 Keith Windschuttle, 'The Secret World of Academia', *Quadrant*, 29 June 2018, p. 3.

82 Stefan Collini, *What Are Universities For?*, p. 66.

83 Jonathan Rauch, *The Constitution of Knowledge*, p. 61.

84 Rauch, *The Constitution of Knowledge*, p. 90.

85 Rauch, *The Constitution of Knowledge*, p. 110.

86 Greg Sheridan, 'The West's Civil Disobedience – It's a Trend to Die For',
The Australian, 26 March 2020.

87 Robert French, *Report of the Independent Review of Freedom of Speech in
Australian Higher Education Providers*, March 2019.

88 Sally Walker, *Review of the Adoption of the Model Code on Freedom of Speech and
Academic Freedom*, December 2020.

89 Alan Tudge, Speech to the Universities Australia Higher Education Conference,
Canberra, 3 June 2021

90 Alan Tudge, Speech to the Universities Australia Higher Education Conference.

91 Watts, 'What Crisis of Academic Freedom?', p. 14.

92 Anthony Galloway, '"Real Risk of Censorship" in Grants Process', *The Sydney
Morning Herald*, 3 April 2021.

93 Robert Bolton, 'Funding for Basic Research Disappears', *Australian Financial
Review*, 24 June 2019.

94 Collini, *What are Universities For?*, p. 75.

95   Raewyn Connell, *The Good University*, Melbourne: Monash University
      Publishing, 2019, p. 32.

96   Rauch, *The Constitution of Knowledge*, p. 194.

97   Searle, 'Rationality and Realism', p. 66.

5: Ambition

1   Silja Baller, Soumitra Datta and Bruno Lanvin (eds), The Global Information
      Technology Report 2016, Geneva: World Economic Forum, 2016, p. 4.

2   Enrico Deiaco, Alan Hughes and Maureen McKelvey, 'Universities as Strategic
      Actors in the Knowledge Economy', *Cambridge Journal of Economics*, 36, 2012,
      p. 526.

3   Deiaco, Hughes and McKelvey, 'Universities as Strategic Actors in the
      Knowledge Economy'.

4   Anders Brostrum, Guido Buenstorf, and Maureen McKelvey, 'The Knowledge
      Economy, Innovation, and the New Challenges to Universities', *Innovation,
      Organisation and Management*, 23:2, 2021, p. 150.

5   Brostrum, Buenstorf and McKelvey, 'The Knowledge Economy, Innovation, and
      the New Challenges to Universities'.

6   Glyn Davis, *The Australian Idea of a University*.

7   Ben R. Martin, 'Are Universities and University Research Under Threat?
      Towards an Evolutionary Model of University Speciation', *Cambridge Journal of
      Economics*, 36, 2012, p. 546.

8   Martin, 'Are Universities and University Research Under Threat?', pp. 550–52.

9   Peter Drucker, *The Age of Discontinuity: Guidelines to Our Changing Society*,
      New York: Harper and Row, 1969.

10   Barry Jones, *Science and Technology Policy*, Sydney: Australian Labor Party,
      1983, INLA Npf 32429407 A938.

11   Interview with John Dawkins, Eden Valley, 3 June 2022.

12   Christopher Freeman, *Technology Policy and Economic Performance: Lessons
      From Japan*, London: Pinter, 1987.

13   Eugene B. Skolnikoff, 'Knowledge without Borders? Internationalisation of the
      Research Universities', *Daedalus*, 122:4, Fall 1993, p. 227.

14   Brostrum, Buenstorf and McKelvey, 'The Knowledge Economy, Innovation, and
      the New Challenges to Universities', p. 145.

15   Linda Weiss, *America Inc? Innovation and Enterprise in the National Security
      State*, New York: Cornell University Press, 2014.

16   For example, Tim Dodd, 'Universities Call for Funding to Arrest Slump in R&D',
      The Australian, 12 July 2018.

17   Interview with Brendan Nelson, Canberra, 17 August 2022.

18   Australian Government, *Backing Australia's Ability: An Innovation Action Plan
      for the Future*, Canberra: Commonwealth of Australia, 2001, p. 3.

19   Robert Bolton, 'Universities Extend a Helping Hand', *Australian Financial
      Review*, 3 October 2020.

20   Dan Tehan, 'Foreword', *The Australian*, 23 September 2020.

21   Tim Dodd, 'Education Faces Tests in a World of Change', *The Australian*, 31 March 2021.

22   For example, Tim Dodd, 'Odd How These Post-truth Institutions Turned Out to Be Right All Along', *The Australian*, 24 February 2021.

23   For example, letters, *The Age*, 15 April 2020.

24   Baller, Datta and Lanvin (eds), *The Global Information Technology Report*, p. xxi.

25   Hannah Forsyth, 'Expanding Higher Education, pp. 368–69.

26   Nicholas Reece, 'How to Foster an Australian Elon Musk', *The Age*, 6 February 2021.

27   Roy Green, 'Innovation Missing in Economic Future Plans', *Australian Financial Review*, 14 May 2019.

28   Simon Devitt, 'Australia No Longer Leads the World in Quantum Computing', *Australian Financial Review*, 4 August 2021.

29   For example, Ryan Craig, 'Will Universities Miss the Digital Revolution?', *The Australian*, 11 December 2021.

30   Keith Houghton, 'Global Rankings Likely at Risk as Cross-subsidisation Takes a Covid Hit', *The Australian* 15 December 2021

31   Leah Dowlett, 'Global University Rankings and Strategic Planning: A Case Study of Australian Institutional Performance', *Journal of Higher Education Policy and Management*, 42:4, 2020, pp. 478–94.

32   Simon Marginson, 'Global University Rankings: Implications in General and for Australia', *Journal of Higher Education Policy and Management*, 29:2, July 2007, p. 132.

33   Marginson, 'Global University Rankings', p. 136.

34   Julie Hare, 'WA Chief Scientist Pushes for Creation of "Super" University', *Australian Financial Review*, 29 November 2021.

35   Michelle Stack, *Global University Rankings and the Mediatization of Higher Education*, Basingstoke: Macmillan, 2016, p. 4.

36   Marginson, 'Global University Rankings', pp. 131–32.

37   Dowlett, 'Global University Rankings and Strategic Planning'.

38   Marginson, 'Global University Rankings', p. 132.

39   Stack, *Global University Rankings*, p. 14.

40   Dowlett, 'Global University Rankings and Strategic Planning', p. 488.

41   Stack, *Global University Rankings*, p. 10.

42   Tim Dodd, 'Australia's "Big Five" Universities are Pulling Away from the Rest', *The Australian*, 17 August 2022.

43   Julie Hare, 'Australian Unis Rise up Rankings' *Australian Financial Review*, 16 November 2021.

44   For example letters, *The Australian*, 27 February 2021.

45   For example Royce Millar, Farah Tomazin and Adam Carey, 'Failing Grades', *The Age*, 3 April 2021.

46   Anil K. Narayan, Deryl Northcott and Lee D. Parker, 'Managing the

Accountability-Autonomy Tensions in University Research Commercialisation', *Financial Accounting and Management*, 33, 2017, p. 335.

47   Enrico Deiaco, Alan Hughes and Maureen McKelvey, 'Universities as Strategic Actors in the Knowledge Economy', *Cambridge Journal of Economics*, 36, 2012, p. 526.

48   Leeland L. Glenna, 'The Purpose-driven University: The Role of University Research in the Era of Science Commercialisation', *Agriculture and Human Values*, 34, 2017, p. 1021.

49   Nicholas Reece, 'How to Foster an Australian Elon Musk', *The Age*, 6 February 2021.

50   Carsten Murawski, 'We Need to Future-proof the Next Generation of Finance Leaders', *Australian Financial Review*, 12 November 2021.

51   David Swan, 'R&D Strategy Stalls as Investment Flatlines', *The Australian*, 4 September 2021.

52   Mark Zachary Taylor, *The Politics of Innovation*, Oxford: Oxford University Press, 2016.

53   Vannevar Bush, *Science, The Endless Frontier, Report to the President on a Program for Postwar Scientific Research*, Washington: National Science Foundation, 1960 [1945].

54   Brostrum, Buenstorf and McKelvey, 'The Knowledge Economy, Innovation, and the New Challenges to Universities', p. 146.

55   Narayan, Northcott and Parker, 'Managing the Accountability-Autonomy Tensions in University Research Commercialisation', p. 336.

56   Brostrum, Buenstorf and McKelvey, 'The Knowledge Economy, Innovation, and the New Challenges to Universities', p. 147.

57   Tim Dodd, 'Unis with Start-up Spark', *The Australian*, 10 November 2021.

58   Narayan, Northcott and Parker, 'Managing the Accountability-Autonomy Tensions in University Research Commercialisation', p. 336.

59   Narayan, Northcott and Parker, 'Managing the Accountability-Autonomy Tensions in University Research Commercialisation', p.336.

60   Narayan, Northcott and Parker, 'Managing the Accountability-Autonomy Tensions in University Research Commercialisation', p. 338.

61   Deiaco, Hughes and McKelvey, 'Universities as Strategic Actors in the Knowledge Economy', p.526.

62   Narayan, Northcott and Parker, 'Managing the Accountability-Autonomy Tensions in University Research Commercialisation', p. 337.

63   Glenna, 'The Purpose-driven University'.

64   Jane Calvert, 'What's Special about Basic Research?', *Science, Technology and Human Values*, 31:2, March 2006, p. 212.

65   Pierre Bourdieu, 'The Specificity of the Scientific Field and the Social Conditions of the Progress of Reason', *Social Science Information*, 14:6, 1975, pp. 19–47.

66   OECD, *Structural Adjustment and Human Performance*, Paris: OECD, 1987.

67   Moira O'Neill and Sharmistha Bagchi-Sen, 'Public Universities and Human

Capital Development in the United States', *Geojournal*, March 2022, https://link.springer.com/content/pdf/10.1007/s10708-022-10636-1.pdf, accessed 2 February 2023.

68   Interview with John Dawkins, Eden Valley, 3 June 2022.

69   Peter Costello, *Intergenerational Report, 2002–03*, 2002–03 Budget Paper No. 5, Canberra: Commonwealth of Australia, 14 May 2002.

70   Victor Gekara, Darren Snell, Alemayehu Molla, Stan Karanasios and Amanda Thomas, 'Skilling the Australian Workforce for the Digital Economy', NCVER Research Report, Adelaide, NCVER, 2019, p. 21.

71   Jeromy B. Temple and Peter McDonald, 'Is Demography Destiny? The Role of Structural and Demographic Factors in Australia's Past and Future Labour Supply', *Journal of Population Research*, 25:1, 2008, p. 47.

72   Mark Barnaba, 'No Silver Bullet for Skill Shortages', EY Report, 20 October 2021, https://www.ey.com/en_au/economics/no-silver-bullet-for-skill-shortages, accessed 2 February 2023.

73   For example, Greg Brown, 'Mining Students "Being Heckled at Uni"', *The Australian*, 21 January 2021.

74   Julie Hare, 'Call for Work-based Learning at Uni', *Australian Financial Review*, 7 December 2021.

75   Andrew Norton, 'Has Job-ready Graduates Increased the Number of Commencing Students?', 25 March 2021, https://andrewnorton.net.au/2021/03/25/has-job-ready-graduates-increased-the-number-of-commencing-students, accessed 2 February 2023.

76   See for example, Letters, *The Age*, 20 February 2018.

77   Diana Hicks, Paul Wouters, Ludo Waltman, Sarah de Rijcke and Ismael Rafols, 'Bibliometrics: The Leiden Manifesto for Research Metrics', *Nature*, 520: 7548, 22 April 2015, pp. 429–31.

6: Privilege

1   For example, Robert Bolton, 'Unis Should Listen to What Students Want from Their Degrees', *Australian Financial Review*, 25 March 2019.

2   Marginson, *Higher Education and the Common Good*, p. 4.

3   Marginson, *Higher Education and the Common Good*, p. 3.

4   Stuart Macintyre, *Australia's Boldest Experiment: War and Reconstruction in the 1940s*, Sydney: NewSouth Publishing, 2015.

5   Forsyth, 'Expanding Higher Education', p. 366.

6   Forsyth, 'Expanding Higher Education', p. 366.

7   This paragraph draws extensively on Forsyth, 'Expanding Higher Education'.

8   My thanks to Mark Considine for suggesting these labels.

9   Sue Green, 'We Need to Avoid University "Obsession"', *The Age*, 12 June 2020.

10   Forsyth, 'Expanding Higher Education', p. 371.

11   For example, Kim Carr, 'With Quality on the Line, "University" is a Title That Should Not Be Bestowed Lightly', *The Australian*, 7 July 2021.

12   Robert Bolton, 'Dropping Out of University the Right Move for Some Students', *Australian Financial Review*, 7 May 2018.

13   Forsyth, 'Expanding Higher Education', p. 368.

14   Thomas Piketty, *Capital and Ideology*, p. 542.

15   Glyn Davis, *The Australian Idea of a University*, p. 5.

16   See for example Robert Bolton, 'Big-name Uni, Higher-level Degree Pays Off', *Australian Financial Review*, 3 August 2020; Michael Koziol, 'Which Uni to Pick to Get Best Wages', *The Age*, 31 October 2018.

17   Damon Kitney, '"Narrow" schooling behind top CEOs', *The Australian*, 10 May 2019.

18   Krzysztof Czarnecki, 'Less Inequality Through Universal Access? Socioeconomic Background of Tertiary Entrants in Australia after the Expansion of University Participation', *Higher Education*, 76, 2018, p. 503.

19   Richard Gluyas, 'Lessons from University of Two Hard Knocks', *The Australian*, 11 June 2020.

20   Letters, *The Australian*, 7 August 2020.

21   Fred Hirsch, *The Social Limits to Growth*, London: Routledge and Kegan Paul, 1977.

22   Marginson, *Higher Education and the Common Good*, p. 207.

23   Marginson, 'Global University Rankings', p. 140.

24   My thanks to Andrew Norton for this point.

25   Marginson, 'Global University Rankings', p. 503

26   Simon Marginson, 'Global University Rankings: Implications in General and for Australia', *Journal of Higher Education Policy and Management*, 29:2, July 2007, p. 132.

27   For example Henrietta Cook, Craig Butt and Maggy Liu, 'It's Harder to Find a Place at University', *The Age*, 17 January 2018.

28   Marginson, *Higher Education and the Common Good*, p. 206.

29   Simon Marginson, 'Equity, Status and Freedom', p. 31.

30   Samuel R. Lucas, 'Effectively Maintained Inequality: Education Transitions, Track Mobility, and Social Background Effects', *American Journal of Sociology*, 106:6, May 2001, pp. 1642–90; Czarnecki, 'Less Inequality Through Universal Access?', p. 502.

31   Brendan Cantwell, 'High Participation Systems of Higher Education' in Brendan Cantwell, Simon Marginson and Anna Smolentseva (eds), *High Participation Systems of Higher Education*, Oxford: Oxford University Press, 2018, p. 27.

32   Interview with John Dawkins, Eden Valley, 3 June 2022.

33   Interview with David Kemp, Melbourne, 15 July 2022.

34   Marginson, *Higher Education and the Common Good*, p. 212.

35   Marginson, 'Global University Rankings', p. 134.

36   Marginson, *Higher Education and the Common Good*, p. 208.

37   Marginson, *Educating Australia*, p. 34.

38   Interview with John Dawkins, Eden Valley, 3 June 2022.

39   John Dawkins, *Higher Education: A Policy Statement*, p. 20.

40   *Towards a Fairer Australia: Social Justice Under Labor*, Canberra: AGPS, 1988.

41   Dawkins, *Higher Education: A Policy Statement*, p. 21.

42   Department of Education, Employment and Training, *A Fair Chance for All: National and Institutional Planning for Equity in Higher Education: A Discussion Paper*, Canberra: AGPS, 1990.

43   Department of Education, Employment and Training, *A Fair Chance for All*, p. 2.

44   Department of Education, Employment and Training, *A Fair Chance for All*, p. 7.

45   Department of Education, Employment and Training, *A Fair Chance for All*, p. vi.

46   Department of Education, Employment and Training, *A Fair Chance for All*, p. 8.

47   Bradley, Noonan, Nugent and Scales, *Review of Australian Higher Education, Final Report*, Canberra: Commonwealth of Australia, 2008, p. xii.

48   Bradley, Noonan, Nugent and Scales, *Review of Australian Higher Education*, p. 27.

49   National Centre for Student Equity in Higher Education data set, NCHSE website: https://www.ncsehe.edu.au/national-data, accessed 2 February 2023.

50   Beni Cakitaki, Michael Luckman and Andrew Harvey, *Equity Off Course: Mapping Equity Access Across Courses and Institutions*, National Centre for Student Equity in Higher Education, Perth: Curtin University, 2022.

51   Marginson, *Higher Education and the Common Good*, p. 245.

52   Tim Pitman, 'Understanding "Fairness" in Student Selection: Are There Differences and Does It Make a Difference Anyway?', *Studies in Higher Education*, 41:7, 2016, p. 1209.

53   Pitman, 'Understanding "Fairness" in Student Selection'.

54   Marginson, *Higher Education and the Common Good*, p. 247.

55   Bradley, Noonan, Nugent and Scales, *Review of Australian Higher Education*, p. 38.

56   Pitman, 'Understanding "Fairness" in Student Selection', pp. 1208–09.

57   Interview with a university recruiter, quoted in Michael Cuthill and Christopher Schmidt, 'Widening Participation: Challenges Confronting a Research-Intensive University', *Journal of Institutional Research*, 16:2, December 2011.

58   Cuthill and Schmidt, 'Widening Participation'.

59   Marginson, 'Equity, Status and Freedom', p. 32.

60   Marginson, *Higher Education and the Common Good*, p. 226.

61   Pierre Bourdieu, *Homo Academicus*, Stanford: Stanford University Press, 1990.

62   Kate Bone, 'Home Life on Hold as Universities Exploit Staff', *The Age*, 10 June 2019.

63   Damian Cahill, 'Wage Theft is the Uni Sector's Dirty Little Secret', *Australian Financial Review*, 18 October 2021.

64   Nour Dados, James Goodman and Keiko Yasukawa, 'Counting the Uncounted: Contestations Over Casualisation Data in Australian Universities', in Jeff Evans, Sally Ruane and Humphrey Southall (eds), *Data in Society: Challenging Statistics in an Age of Globalisation*, Bristol: Bristol University Press, 2019, p. 330.

65   Megan Kimber, 'The Tenured "Core" and the Tenuous "Periphery": The Casualisation of Academic Work in Australian Universities', *Journal of Higher Education Policy and Management*, 25:1, May 2003, p. 46.

66   Kimber, 'The Tenured "Core" and the Tenuous "Periphery"'.

67   Julie Hare, '"Systemic" Uni Wage Theft "Out of Control"', *Australian Financial Review*, 21 October 2021.

68   Robert Bolton, 'Bloated Student to Staff Ratios the Dark Secret of Tertiary Sector', *Australian Financial Review*, 13 July 2020.

69   Natasha Abrahams, 'Kudos but Little Cash for the Postgraduates Who Lift University Rankings', *The Australian*, 26 June 2019.

70   Archie Thomas, Hannah Forsyth and Andrew G. Bonnell, '"The Dice Are Loaded": History, Solidarity and Precarity in Australian Universities', *History Australia*, 17:1, 2020, p. 24.

71   Kimber, 'The Tenured "Core" and the Tenuous "Periphery"', p. 44.

72   Greg McCarthy, Xianlin Song and Kanishka Jayasuriya, 'The Proletarianisation of Academic Labour in Australia', *Higher Education Research and Development*, 36:5, 2017, p. 1020.

73   Kimber, 'The Tenured "Core" and the Tenuous "Periphery"', p. 46.

74   Quoted in Dados, Goodman and Yasukawa, 'Counting the Uncounted', p. 331.

75   See for example Anna Prytz, 'University Apologises Over Casuals' Wage Theft', *The Age*, 10 September 2021.

76   Marginson, *Higher Education and the Common Good*, p. 244.

77   Piketty, *Capital and Ideology*, p. 812.

78   Piketty, *Capital and Ideology*, p. 773.

79   Nick Cater, *The Lucky Culture and the Rise of an Australian Ruling Class*, p. 27.

80   Interview with Lindsay Tanner, Melbourne, 14 June 2022.

81   Paul Kelly, *The End of Certainty*.

82   Tim Dymond, 'A History of the "New Class" Concept in Australian Public Discourse' in Marian Sawer and Barry Hindess (eds), *Us and Them: Anti-Elitism in Australia*, Perth: API Network, 2004, p. 58.

83   Dymond, 'A History of the "New Class" Concept in Australian Public Discourse', pp. 98–99.

84   Piketty, *Capital and Ideology*, p. 1008.

85   Steve Mickler, 'Talkback Radio, Anti-Elitism and Moral Decline: A Fatal Paradox?' in Sawer and Hindess (eds), *Us and Them: Anti-Elitism in Australia*, pp. 98–99

86   Robert Menzies, 'Australian Universities: Ministerial Statement in Connexion with the Report of the Committee', 28 November 1957, Canberra: AGPS.

87   Bri Lee, 'Correspondence', p. 137.

88   Michael J. Sandel, *The Tyranny of Merit: What's Become of the Common Good?*, London: Allen Lane, 2020, p. 95

89   Barry Hindess and Marian Sawer, 'Introduction' in Sawer and Hindess (eds), *Us and Them: Anti-Elitism in Australia*, pp. 1–2.

Conclusion: Transformation

1   My thanks to Andrew Norton for sending me time series data on opinion about universities.

2   Marginson, *Higher Education and the Common Good*, p. 225.

3   Slaughter and Leslie, *Academic Capitalism: Politics, Policies and the Entrepreneurial University*.

4   J. Maloney, quoted in Sharon Andrews, 'Why Are We Whispering? Academic Freedom in Australia: An Arendtian Analysis', *Critical Studies in Education*, 43:1, 2002, p. 50.

5   W. J. Baumol and Sue-Anne Baty-Blackman, 'How to Think about Rising College Costs', *Planning for Higher Education*, 23, 1995, pp. 1–7.

6   Michael J. Sandel, *What Money Can't Buy*, London: Penguin Books, 2012, p. 34.

7   Sandel, *What Money Can't Buy*, pp. 90–91.

8   My thanks to Robert Manne for making this point.

9   My thanks to Andrew Norton for this point.

10   My thanks to Adrian Little for this point.

11   Tanya Plibersek, Speech to the *Australian Financial Review* Higher Education Conference, Sydney, 16 August 2021.

12   Marginson, 'Equity, Status and Freedom', p. 32.

INDEX